AAT

Level 2

Certificate in Accounting

Introduction to Bookkeeping

Question Bank

For assessments from September 2022

First edition 2021

ISBN 9781 5097 4120 5
eISBN 9781 5097 4178 6

British Library Cataloguing-in-Publication Data
A catalogue record for this book is available from the
British Library

Published by

BPP Learning Media Ltd
BPP House, Aldine Place
142-144 Uxbridge Road
London W12 8AA

www.bpp.com/learningmedia

Printed in the United Kingdom

Your learning materials, published by BPP Learning
Media Ltd, are printed on paper obtained from
traceable sustainable sources.

Contents

Introduction

Introduction

This is BPP Learning Media's AAT Question Bank for *Introduction to Bookkeeping*. It is part of a suite of ground-breaking resources produced by BPP Learning Media for AAT assessments.

This Question Bank has been written in conjunction with the BPP Course Book, and has been carefully designed to enable students to practise all of the learning outcomes and assessment criteria for the units that make up *Introduction to Bookkeeping*. It is fully up to date as at November 2021 and reflects both AAT's qualification specification and the practice assessments provided by AAT.

This Question Bank contains these key features:

- Tasks corresponding to each chapter of the Course Book. Some tasks are designed for learning purposes, others are of assessment standard

- Further BPP practice assessments

The emphasis in all tasks and assessments is on the practical application of the skills acquired.

VAT

You may find tasks throughout this Question Bank that need you to calculate or be aware of a rate of VAT. This is stated at 20% in these examples and questions.

Approaching the assessment

When you sit the assessment it is very important that you follow the on screen instructions. This means you need to carefully read the instructions, both on the introduction screens and during specific tasks.

When you access the assessment you should be presented with an introductory screen with information similar to that shown below (taken from the introductory screen from AAT's Q2022 practice assessment 1 for *Introduction to Bookkeeping*).

You have **1 hour and 30 minutes** to complete this sample assessment.

- This assessment contains **11 tasks** and you should attempt to complete **every** task.
- Each task is independent. You will not need to refer to your answers to previous tasks.
- The total number of marks for this assessment is **100**.
- Read every task carefully to make sure you understand what is required.
- Where the date is relevant, it is given in the task data.
- Both minus signs and brackets can be used to indicate negative numbers **unless** task instructions state otherwise.
- You must use a full stop to indicate a decimal point. For example, write 100.57 **not** 100,57 or 10057.
- You may use a comma to indicate a number in the thousands, but you don't have to. For example, 10000 and 10,000 are both acceptable.

Scenario

The tasks in this assessment are set in different business situations where the following apply:

- Businesses use a variety of bookkeeping systems.
- Double entry takes place in the general ledger.
- The VAT rate is 20%.

The actual instructions will vary depending on the subject you are studying for. It is very important you read the instructions on the introductory screen and apply them in the assessment. You don't want to lose marks when you know the correct answer just because you have not entered it in the right format.

In general, the rules set out in the AAT practice assessments for the subject you are studying for will apply in the real assessment, but you should carefully read the information on this screen again in the real assessment, just to make sure. This screen may also confirm the VAT rate used if applicable.

A full stop is needed to indicate a decimal point. We would recommend using minus signs to indicate negative numbers and leaving out the comma signs to indicate thousands, as this results in a lower number of key strokes and less margin for error when working under time pressure. Having said that, you can use whatever is easiest for you as long as you operate within the rules set out for your particular assessment.

You have to show competence throughout the assessment and you should therefore complete all of the tasks. Don't leave questions unanswered.

When asked to fill in tables, or gaps, never leave any blank even if you are unsure of the answer. Fill in your best estimate.

Note. that for some assessments where there is a lot of scenario information or tables of data provided, you may need to access these via 'pop-ups'. Instructions will be provided on how you can bring up the necessary data during the assessment.

Finally, take note of any task specific instructions once you are in the assessment. For example you may be asked to enter a date in a certain format or to enter a number to a certain number of decimal places.

Grading

To achieve the qualification and to be awarded a grade, you must pass all the mandatory unit assessments, all optional unit assessments (where applicable) and the synoptic assessment.

The AAT Level 2 Foundation Certificate in Accounting will be awarded a grade. This grade will be based on performance across the qualification. Unit assessments and synoptic assessments are not individually graded. These assessments are given a mark that is used in calculating the overall grade.

How overall grade is determined

You will be awarded an overall qualification grade (Distinction, Merit, and Pass). If you do not achieve the qualification you will not receive a qualification certificate, and the grade will be shown as unclassified.

The marks of each assessment will be converted into a percentage mark and rounded up or down to the nearest whole number. This percentage mark is then weighted according to the weighting of the unit assessment or synoptic assessment within the qualification. The resulting weighted assessment percentages are combined to arrive at a percentage mark for the whole qualification.

Grade definition	Percentage threshold
Distinction	90–100%
Merit	80–89%
Pass	70–79%
Unclassified	0–69% Or failure to pass one or more assessment/s

Re-sits

Some AAT qualifications such as the AAT Foundation Certificate in Accounting have restrictions in place for how many times you are able to re-sit assessments. Please refer to the AAT website for further details.

You should only be entered for an assessment when you are well prepared and you expect to pass the assessment.

AAT qualifications

The material in this book may support the following AAT qualifications:

AAT Level 2 Certificate in Accounting, AAT Level 2 Certificate in Bookkeeping, and AAT Certificate in Accounting at SCQF Level 6.

Supplements

From time to time we may need to publish supplementary materials to one of our titles. This can be for a variety of reasons. From a small change in the AAT unit guidance to new legislation coming into effect between editions.

You should check our supplements page regularly for anything that may affect your learning materials. All supplements are available free of charge on our supplements page on our website at:

www.bpp.com/learning-media/about/students

Improving material and removing errors

There is a constant need to update and enhance our study materials in line with both regulatory changes and new insights into the assessments.

From our team of authors BPP appoints a subject expert to update and improve these materials for each new edition.

Their updated draft is subsequently technically checked by another author and from time to time non-technically checked by a proof reader.

We are very keen to remove as many numerical errors and narrative typos as we can but given the volume of detailed information being changed in a short space of time we know that a few errors will sometimes get through our net.

We apologise in advance for any inconvenience that an error might cause. We continue to look for new ways to improve these study materials and would welcome your suggestions. If you have any comments about this book, please email nisarahmed@bpp.com or write to Nisar Ahmed, AAT Head of Programme, BPP Learning Media Ltd, BPP House, Aldine Place, London W12 8AA.

Question Bank

Chapter 1 – Business documentation

The tasks in this Question Bank are set in different business situations where the following apply:

- Businesses use a variety of bookkeeping systems.
- Double entry takes place in the general ledger.
- The VAT rate is 20%.

Task 1.1

For each of the following transactions state whether they are cash or credit transactions:

	Cash transaction ✓	Credit transaction ✓
Purchase of goods for £200 payable by cash in one week's time	✓	
Writing a cheque for the purchase of a new computer	✓	
Sale of goods to a customer where the invoice accompanies the goods		
Receipt of a cheque from a customer for goods purchased today		
Purchase of goods where payment is due in three weeks' time		

Task 1.2

When a supplier delivers goods to a customer, the customer will expect to receive in due course:

✓	
	A credit note
	A remittance advice
	A petty cash voucher
✓	An invoice

BPP
LEARNING
MEDIA

Task 1.3

A customer wishes to return faulty goods to a credit supplier.

Which document should the customer send with the return?

	✓	
	✓	A credit note
		A goods received note
		A goods returned note
		An invoice

Task 1.4

Freddie wishes to purchase some desks from Joe, his credit supplier.

(a) **Which document should Joe issue to Freddie at each stage of this sales process?**

	Document issued by Joe
Freddie asks Joe for a quote on the cost of 14 desks	Quat ▼
Joe delivers 14 desks to Freddie	Delivery note ▼
Joe requests payment from Freddie	Invoice ▼
Freddie pays his invoice and takes a prompt payment discount	Remitance ▼

Picklist:

Credit note
Customer order
Delivery note
Goods received note
Goods returned note
Invoice
Quotation
Remittance advice

(b) **Which document should Freddie create at each stage of the purchase process?**

	Document created by Freddie
Freddie places an order with Joe for 14 desks	Purchase Order ▼
Freddie accepts in to his warehouse delivery of 14 desks from Joe	Good Received ▼
Freddie returns one faulty desk to Joe	Credit Note ▼
Freddie pays his invoice	Rem / Sadl ▼

4

Picklist:

Credit note
Customer order
Delivery note
Goods received note
Goods returned note
Invoice
Purchase order
Remittance advice
Sales order

Task 1.5

Ken trades in exotic dress materials. He has a large number of small suppliers. He likes to keep all invoices and credit notes from each supplier together in a file for that supplier.

Which sort of coding system would be most appropriate for Ken to use when devising a unique code number for each supplier?

✓	
✓	An alphanumerical system
	A numerical system

Task 1.6

JMC Ltd allocates a customer code to each of its customers as shown below. The codes are made up of the first two letters of the customer's name, followed by the number of the ledger page allocated to each customer in that alphabetical group.

Customer name	Customer code
Baxters Ltd	Ba01
Britoil	Br02
Drumbuie Ltd	Dr01
Drumchapel Ltd	Dr02
Joulie Walker	Jo01
Walkers Ltd	Wa01
William Grant Ltd	Wi02
Whyte and Mackay	Wh03

JMC Ltd has two new credit customers which need to be allocated a customer code.

Insert the relevant customer codes for each customer.

Customer	Customer code
Caledonian Ltd	Ca01
Jury's Brewery Ltd	Ju01

BPP
LEARNING
MEDIA

Task 1.7

Complete the sentence

In order to identify how much is owed to a supplier at any point in time, purchases invoices are coded with a:

▼

Picklist:

Customer code
General ledger code
Product code
Supplier code

Task 1.8

Sumberton Ltd codes all purchase invoices with a supplier code **and** a general ledger code. A selection of the codes used is given below.

Supplier	Supplier Code
Casaubon's	PL012
Frankie's Leatherware	PL128
Jane Peel Ltd	PL244
Trinder and Papp	PL301
Wishburton Ltd	PL666

Item	General Ledger Code
Leather bags	GL001
Canvas bags	GL002
Wheeled cases	GL003
Carry cases	GL004
Accessories	GL005

This is an invoice received from a supplier.

Jane Peel Ltd **56 Ward End Road, Doristown DO9 3YU** **VAT Registration No. 134 1452 22**

Sumberton Ltd
Sumberton House
10 Main Road
Sawlow
SA7 5LD

23 December 20XX

	£
10 leather bags (product code R245L) @ £17.50 each	175.00
VAT @ 20%	35.00
Total	210.00

(a) **Select which codes would be used to code this invoice.**

Supplier code	▼
General ledger code	▼

Picklist:

GL001
GL002
GL003
GL004
GL005
PL012
PL128
PL244
PL301
PL666

(b) **Complete the sentence.**

In order to identify how much has been spent on a particular product for resale at any point in time, purchases invoices are coded with a

▼

.

Picklist:

Customer code
General ledger code
Product code
Supplier code

Task 1.9

Ken trades in exotic dress materials. He codes all purchase invoices with a supplier code **and** a general ledger code. A selection of the codes used is given below.

Supplier	Supplier Code
Henderson Co	HEN562
Mack Materials	MAC930
Vinceroy Ltd	VIN234
Streamers	STR220
AVR Partners	AVR001

Product	General Ledger Code
Lace	GL501
Calico	GL502
Seersucker	GL503
Cambric	GL504
Velvet	GL505

This is an invoice received from a supplier.

Vinceroy Ltd
17 Fall Road, Agburton AG5 2WE
VAT Registration No. 783 2873 33
Invoice number: 892

Ken's Exotics
1 Bath Street 5 Feb 20XX
Cembury, CE11 9SD

	£
20 metres .... Velvet @ £7.00 per metre	140.00
VAT @ 20%	28.00
Total	168.00

(a)   **Select which codes would be used to code this invoice.**

Supplier account code	▼
General ledger code	▼

Picklist:

AVR001
GL501
GL502
GL503
GL504
GL505
HEN562
MAC930
STR220
VIN234

(b) **Why is it necessary to use a general ledger code?**

Picklist:
To help trace relevant accounts quickly and easily.
To make sure the correct balances are calculated.
To prevent fraud.

Chapter 2 – The books of prime entry

Task 2.1

Kendo Ltd trades in exotic dress materials. On 7 August, he is preparing an invoice for goods of £100 plus VAT, for a customer, VXT Ltd.

What will be the amounts entered in the sales daybook when the invoice has been prepared?

Sales daybook

Date 20XX	Details	Invoice number	Total £	VAT £	Net £
7 August	▼	172			

Picklist:

Kendo Ltd
VXT Ltd

Task 2.2

Kendo has prepared the following invoice.

Kendo Ltd
VAT Registration number 369 4453 00
Invoice No. 365

To: R Hart	15 June 20XX	
		£
450 product code MM12 @ £1.20 each		540.00
VAT @ 20%		108.00
Total		648.00
Terms: Net monthly account		

How will this invoice be entered in to Kendo Ltd's sales daybook?

Sales daybook

Date 20XX	Details	Invoice number	Total £	VAT £	Net £
15 June	▼				

Picklist:

Kendo Ltd
R Hart

Task 2.3

Natural Productions is a small business that manufactures a variety of soaps and bath products which it sells directly to shops. During January 20XX the following credit sales to customers took place:

Invoice No. 6237 to Hoppers Ltd £547 plus VAT

Invoice No. 6238 to Body Perfect £620 plus VAT

Invoice No. 6239 to Esporta Leisure £346 plus VAT

Invoice No. 6240 to Langans Beauty £228 plus VAT

Invoice No. 6241 to Body Perfect £548 plus VAT

Invoice No. 6242 to Superior Products £221 plus VAT

Invoice No. 6243 to Esporta Leisure £416 plus VAT

Invoice No. 6244 to Hoppers Ltd £238 plus VAT

Invoice No. 6245 to Langans Beauty £274 plus VAT

You are required to:

(a)   Enter these transactions into the sales daybook given below.

(b)   Cast the columns of the sales daybook and check that they cross cast.

Sales daybook

Customer	Invoice number	Total £	VAT £	Net £
▼	6237			
▼	6238			
▼	6239			
▼	6240			
▼	6241			
▼	6242			
▼	6243			
▼	6244			
▼	6245			

Picklist:

Body Perfect
Esporta Leisure
Hoppers Ltd
Langans Beauty
Natural Productions
Superior Products

Cross-cast check:

	£
Net	
VAT	
Total	

Task 2.4

During January the following credit notes were issued by Natural Productions to various customers:

Credit note No. 1476 to Hoppers Ltd £68.70 plus VAT

Credit note No. 1477 to Esporta Leisure £89.20 plus VAT

Credit note No. 1478 to Superior Products £11.75 plus VAT

Record the credit notes in the appropriate daybook by:

- Selecting the correct daybook title and
- Making the necessary entries.

Daybook:	▼

Picklist:

Purchases daybook
Purchases returns daybook
Sales daybook
Sales returns daybook

Customer	Credit note number	Total £	VAT £	Net £
▼	1476			
▼	1477			
▼	1478			

Picklist:

Esporta Leisure
Hoppers Ltd
Natural Productions
Superior Products

Task 2.5

Natural Productions manufactures a variety of soaps and bath products. It buys materials for the manufacturing process from a number of suppliers on credit. It also buys other items such as stationery on credit. During January 20XX Natural Productions received the following invoices from credit suppliers:

P J Phillips	
VAT Registration number 436 4472 01	
Invoice No. 03576	
To: Natural Products	4 Jan 20XX
	£
225 soap dispensers	357.00
VAT @ 20%	71.40
Total	428.40
Terms: Net monthly account	

W J Jones	
VAT Registration number 564 4432 89	
Invoice No. 18435	
To: Natural Products	6 Jan 20XX
	£
Stationery	210.00
VAT @ 20%	42.00
Total	252.00
Terms: Net monthly account	

Record the invoices in the appropriate daybook by:

- Selecting the correct daybook title and
- Making the necessary entries.

Daybook:	▼

Picklist:

Discounts allowed daybook
Discounts received daybook
Purchases daybook
Purchases returns daybook
Sales daybook
Sales returns daybook

Date	Supplier	Invoice number	Total £	VAT £	Purchases (materials) £	Stationery £
	▼					
	▼					

Picklist:

Natural Productions
P J Phillips
W J Jones

Task 2.6

Natural Productions manufactures a variety of soaps and bath products. It buys materials for the manufacturing process from a number of suppliers on credit. It also buys other items such as stationery and packaging on credit. During January 20XX Natural Productions received the following invoices from credit suppliers:

12 Jan Invoice No. 03598 from P J Phillips £413 plus VAT for materials

16 Jan Invoice No. 28423 from Packing Supplies £268 plus VAT for packaging

19 Jan Invoice No. 18478 from Trenter Ltd £521 plus VAT for materials

20 Jan Invoice No. 84335 from O & P Ltd £624 plus VAT for materials

24 Jan Invoice No. 28444 from Packing Supplies £164 plus VAT for packaging

28 Jan Invoice No. 18491 from Trenter Ltd £368 plus VAT for materials

31 Jan Invoice No. 43681 from W J Jones £104 plus VAT for stationery

Record the invoices in the appropriate daybook by:

- **Selecting the correct daybook title and**
- **Making the necessary entries.**

Daybook:	▼

Picklist:

Discounts allowed daybook
Discounts received daybook
Purchases daybook
Purchases returns daybook
Sales daybook
Sales returns daybook

Date	Supplier	Invoice number	Total £	VAT £	Purchases (materials) £	Stationery £	Packaging £
12 Jan	▼	03598					
16 Jan	▼	28423					
19 Jan	▼	18478					
20 Jan	▼	84335					
24 Jan	▼	28444					
28 Jan	▼	18491					
31 Jan	▼	43681					

Picklist:

Natural Productions
O & P Ltd
Packing Supplies
P J Phillips
Trenter Ltd
W J Jones

Task 2.7

During January Natural Productions received the following credit notes from suppliers.

<table>
<tr><td>

P J Phillips

VAT Registration number 436 4472 01
Credit note No. 04216

To: Natural Products   10 Jan 20XX

	£
Materials	98.00
VAT @ 20%	19.60
Total	117.60

Terms: Net monthly account

</td><td>

W J Jones

VAT Registration number 564 4432 89
Credit note No. CN 0643

To: Natural Products   16 Jan 20XX

	£
Stationery	56.00
VAT @ 20%	11.20
Total	67.20

Terms: Net monthly account

</td></tr>
</table>

Record the credit notes in the appropriate daybook by:

- Selecting the correct daybook title and
- Making the necessary entries.

Daybook:	▼

Picklist:

Discounts allowed daybook
Discounts received daybook
Purchases daybook
Purchases returns daybook
Sales daybook
Sales returns daybook

Date	Supplier	Credit note number	Total £	VAT £	Purchases (materials) £	Stationery £	Packaging £
10 Jan	▼	▼					
16 Jan	▼	▼					

Picklist:

Natural Productions
P J Phillips
W J Jones
04216
CN 0643

Task 2.8

You work in the accounts department of Southfield Electrical. You have been given the two credit notes below.

Southfield Electrical	
VAT Registration number 569 5242 89	
Credit note No. 08650	
Customer No. RL 44	21 Sept 20XX
To: Whitehill Superstores	
	£
Zanpoint fridge	330.00
Less 10% trade discount	33.00
	297.00
VAT @ 20%	59.40
Total	356.40
Reason: damaged goods	

Southfield Electrical	
VAT Registration number 569 5242 89	
Credit note No. 08651	
Customer No. RL 15	23 Sept 20XX
To: Dagwell Enterprises	
	£
6 Temax coffee maker	
@ 40.00 each	240.00
Less 15% trade discount	36.00
	204.00
VAT @ 20%	40.80
Total	244.80
Reason: goods not ordered	

Complete the sales returns daybook by:

- Entering the credit notes.
- Totalling the columns.

Sales returns daybook

Date	Customer	Credit note number	Customer code	Gross total £	VAT £	Net £
21 Sep	▼		▼			
23 Sep	▼		▼			
	Totals					

Picklist:

Dagwell Enterprises
Southfield Electrical
Whitehill Superstores
RL 15
RL 44

Task 2.9

Given below are the only four purchase invoices received by Short Furniture in the week ending 27 January 20XX. You are also given an extract from the supplier codes listing.

27 Jan Invoice No. 09642 from Ephraim Supplies £291.00 plus VAT for wood

27 Jan Invoice No. 06932 from Cavendish Woods £705.10 plus VAT for wood

27 Jan Invoice No. 67671 from Calverley Bros £145.60 plus VAT for polish

27 Jan Invoice No. 36004 from Culverden & Co £57.40 plus VAT for other purchases

Supplier codes listing

Calverley Bros   PL03
Cavendish Woods   PL14
Culverden & Co   PL23
Ephraim Supplies   PL39

Complete the purchases daybook by:

- Entering the invoices – note that purchases are analysed into wood, polish and other.
- Totalling the columns.

Purchases daybook

Date	Supplier	Invoice number	Supplier code	Total £	VAT £	Net £	Wood Purchases £	Polish purchases £	Other purchases £
	▼		▼						
	▼		▼						
	▼		▼						
	▼		▼						

Picklist:

Calverley Bros
Cavendish Woods
Culverden & Co
Ephraim Supplies
PL03
PL14
PL23
PL39

Task 2.10

You work for Smith & Co. Credit notes to customers have been prepared and partially entered in the sales returns daybook, as shown below.

(a) Complete the entries in the sales returns daybook by inserting the appropriate figures for each credit note.

(b) Total the last five columns of the sales returns daybook.

Sales returns daybook

Date 20XX	Details	Credit note number	Total £	VAT £	Net £	Bags returns £	Suitcases returns £
30 Nov	Shrier Goods	562		104		520	
30 Nov	Gringles Co	563	408				340
30 Nov	Lester plc	564	1,068		890	890	
	Totals						

Chapter 3 – VAT and discounts

Task 3.1

Ken trades in exotic dress materials. He has many credit customers who operate in the same trade as him and he routinely offers these customers a discount off the list price of his goods in order to maintain good relations.

What type of discount is this an example of?

✓	
✓	A trade discount
	A prompt payment discount
	A bulk discount

Task 3.2

VAT is a tax on consumer expenditure which a VAT registered business must collect from its customers.

Who is VAT paid over to?

✓	
	The Home Office
	The Treasury
	The Inland Revenue
✓	HM Revenue & Customs

Task 3.3

On your desk is a pile of sales invoices that have already had the price of the goods entered onto them and been totalled. The customers are to be given a 15% trade discount.

Calculate the trade discount and net total to be included on each invoice.

Goods total £	Trade discount £	Net total £
416.80		
105.60		
96.40		
263.20		
351.00		

Task 3.4

On your desk there is a pile of invoices which have the net total entered.

Calculate the VAT charge and the invoice total to be included on each invoice.

Net total £	VAT £	Gross total £
258.90	51.78	207.12
316.80		
82.60		
152.70		
451.30		

Task 3.5

The following gross totals include VAT.

Calculate the amount of VAT on each invoice and the net amount of the invoice.

Gross total £	VAT £	Net total £
145.20		
66.90		
246.60		
35.40		
125.40		

Task 3.6

The following purchases have been made for cash inclusive of VAT.

Calculate the amount of VAT on each purchase and the net amount of the purchase.

Gross total £	VAT £	Net total £
252.66		
169.20		
48.60		
104.28		
60.48		
822.60		

Task 3.7

These customers have all been offered a prompt payment discount of 3% if they pay within 10 days.

Calculate the amount each customer would pay if they pay within 10 days and take the prompt payment discount.

Customer	Gross invoice total £	Amount £
J Smith	258	
Anchorage Ltd	312	
VIP Ltd	84	
Blue House Ltd	150	

Task 3.8

A sales invoice is being prepared for goods supplied, as shown in the customer order below. A bulk discount of 2% is given for all orders where more than 100 products have been ordered.

Customer order

> Jules Ltd
> Order number 8965
>
> Please supply: 2 May 20XX
>
> 200 microwaves
>
> @ £35.00 each less 5% trade discount.

Calculate the amounts to be included in the invoice.

	£
Net amount before discounts	
Net amount after discounts	
VAT	
Total	

Task 3.9

An invoice for £1,280 plus VAT has been sent to JKF Ltd offering a prompt payment discount of 10% for payment within 14 days.

(a)   **What is the amount JKF Ltd will pay if they pay within 14 days?**

£ [   ]

JKF Ltd pays the invoice within 14 days and takes the prompt payment discount.

(b) Complete the table below to show the amounts to be included on the credit note for JKF Ltd.

Credit note

Amount	£
Net amount	
VAT	
Gross amount	

Task 3.10

The credit note below has been sent to a customer in respect of a prompt payment discount.

Anchor Supplies Ltd
Horwich Way
Bolton BL8 3XU

VAT Registration No. 424 5242 42

PROMPT PAYMENT DISCOUNT CREDIT NOTE

Shipper Ltd   Customer account code: SHIP001

24 George Street

Rochdale   Invoice no: 298

RC3 4HJ

Credit note no: 223   Date: 15 October 20XX

Net £	VAT £	Gross £
56.00	11.20	67.20

Record the credit note in the appropriate daybook by:

- Selecting the correct daybook title and
- Making the necessary entries.

Daybook:	▼

Picklist:

Discounts allowed daybook
Discounts received daybook
Purchases daybook
Purchases returns daybook
Sales daybook
Sales returns daybook

Date 20XX	Details	Credit note number	Total £	VAT £	Net £
15 Oct	▼	223			

Picklist:

Anchor Supplies Ltd
Shipper Ltd

Task 3.11

The credit note below has been received from a supplier in respect of a prompt payment discount.

<table>
<tr><td colspan="3" align="center">Rent a Van Ltd
31 Cannon Way, Manchester
MZ2 8BS</td></tr>
<tr><td colspan="3" align="center">VAT Registration No. 569 5242 89</td></tr>
<tr><td colspan="3" align="center">PROMPT PAYMENT DISCOUNT CREDIT NOTE</td></tr>
<tr><td colspan="2">Pop Ice Cream ltd</td><td>Customer account code: POP003</td></tr>
<tr><td colspan="2">4 Goodge Street</td><td></td></tr>
<tr><td colspan="2">Ainsworth</td><td>Invoice no: 569</td></tr>
<tr><td colspan="2">Lancs AL52 2FC</td><td></td></tr>
<tr><td colspan="2">Credit note no: 11</td><td>Date: 10 November 20XX</td></tr>
</table>

Net £	VAT £	Gross £
103.00	20.60	123.60

Required

Record the credit note in the appropriate daybook by:

- Selecting the correct daybook title and
- Making the necessary entries.

Daybook:	▼

Picklist:

Discounts allowed daybook
Discounts received daybook
Purchases daybook
Purchases returns daybook
Sales daybook
Sales returns daybook

Date 20XX	Details	Credit note number	Total £	VAT £	Net £
10 Nov	▼	11			

Picklist:

Pop Ice Cream Ltd
Rent a Van Ltd

Task 3.12

An invoice is being prepared by Sumberton Ltd to be sent to Meering Ltd for £2,000 plus VAT. A prompt payment discount of 4% will be offered for payment within 10 days.

(a) **What is the amount Sumberton Ltd should receive if payment is made within 10 days?**

£

(b) **What is the amount Sumberton Ltd should receive if payment is not made within 10 days?**

£

Task 3.13

Sumberton Ltd offers some established customers a discount of 4% whatever the size of their order and irrespective of when they pay.

What is the name of this type of discount?

[▼]

Picklist:

Bulk discount
Prompt payment discount
Trade discount

Task 3.14

Show whether the following statements are true or false.

	True ✓	False ✓
The book of prime entry for discounts allowed is the petty cash book.		✓
Input tax is the VAT suffered on purchases.	✓	
A goods received note is a primary document for recording in the accounting records.	✓	

Chapter 4 – Recording credit sales

Task 4.1

Ken trades in exotic dress materials. A new customer has phoned up with an enquiry about buying some materials from Ken.

What should Ken send the customer?

✓	
	A delivery note
	A price list
	A goods received note
	A statement of account

Task 4.2

Ken wishes to analyse his sales so that he can distinguish between those made to UK customers and those from abroad.

What is the best way for him to do this?

✓	
	Analyse every invoice into a separate column of his analysed sales daybook
	Allocate one of two sales codes to each invoice and use this to write up the invoices in the analysed sales daybook
	Allocate invoice numbers on a randomised basis
	Use a different sequence of invoice numbers for each customer

Task 4.3

On 8 January 20XX, Southfield Electrical received the following purchase order from Whitehill Superstores. The goods were delivered the following day.

Southfield Electrical's customer files show the following information.

Customer name	Customer code	Trade discount	Prompt payment discount
Whitehill Superstores	RL 44	10%	4% – 10 days

BPP
LEARNING
MEDIA

Whitehill Superstores
28 Whitehill Park
Benham DR6 5LM

Purchase Order 32431

Southfield Electrical   4 Jan 20XX
Industrial Estate
Benham DR6 2FF

Please supply 8 units of product code 6260 Hosch Tumble Dryer

@ £300.00 each, plus VAT.

Complete the ten boxes in the sales invoice below.

Southfield Electrical
Industrial Estate
Benham DR6 2FF

VAT registration no: 569 5242 89

SALES INVOICE 57104

Date: [▼]

To: Whitehill Superstores   Customer account code: [ ]
     28 Whitehill Park

     Benham, DR6 5LM   Purchase order no: [ ]

Quantity of units	Product code	Price each £	Total amount after trade discount £	VAT £	Total £

Terms: [▼]

Picklist:

4 Jan 20XX
8 Jan 20XX
9 Jan 20XX
Net monthly account
30 days net
4% prompt payment discount for payment within 10 days
10% trade discount

Task 4.4

On 18 May 20XX, Southfield Electrical received the following purchase order from Harper & Sons Ltd. The goods were delivered the following day.

Southfield Electrical's customer files show the following discount policy.

Customer name	Customer code	Trade discount	Prompt payment discount
Harper & Sons	RL 26	5%	3% – 14 days

Harper & Sons also receives a bulk discount of 5% if the net amount of their order, after deducting trade discount, is over £1,000.

Harper & Sons
30 High Street
Benham DR6 4ST

Purchase Order 04367

Southfield Electrical   16 May 20XX
Industrial Estate
Benham DR6 2FF

Please supply 6 units of product code 6370 Hosch Washing Machine

@ £260.00 each, plus VAT.

Complete the ten boxes in the sales invoice on the following page.

Southfield Electrical
Industrial Estate
Benham DR6 2FF
VAT registration no: 569 5242 89

SALES INVOICE 57105

Date: [19 May 20XX ▼]

To: Harper & Sons   Customer account code: [RL 26]
      30 High Street

      Benham, DR6 4ST   Purchase order no: [04367]

Quantity of units	Product code	Price each £	Total amount after discounts £	VAT £	Total £
6	6370	260.00	1,407.90	273.13	1,681.03

Terms: [Net monthly account ▼]

Picklist:

16 May 20XX
18 May 20XX
19 May 20XX
Net monthly account

30 days net
3% prompt payment discount for payment within 14 days
5% bulk discount
5% trade discount

Task 4.5

On 20 October Whitehill Superstores received an invoice from Southfield Electrical. The invoice is shown below together with the delivery note and the purchase order.

Invoice

Southfield Electrical
Industrial Estate, Benham DR6 2FF
VAT Registration No. 569 5242 89

To: Whitehill Superstores   19 Oct 20XX

Invoice No. 56501

Delivery note 34816
Purchase order 385

	£
15 product 9046 @ £15 each	225.00
VAT @ 20%	45.00
Total	270.00

Terms
Terms: Net monthly account

Delivery note

Southfield Electrical
Industrial Estate, Benham DR6 2FF
VAT Registration No. 569 5242 89

Delivery note 34816

18 Oct 20XX
To:

Whitehill Superstore
28 Whitehill Park
Benham DR6 5LM

Please receive 12 product 9406 Kensharp Toaster.

Purchase order

Whitehill Superstores
Order number 32202

Please supply: 16 Oct 20XX

15 Kensharp Toaster product code 9406

@ £15.00 each less 5% trade discount

As agreed, terms of payment are 3% discount for payment by the end of the month.

(a)   Check the delivery note, the invoice and the purchase order and answer the following questions.

Questions	Yes ✓	No ✓
Has the correct amount of goods been delivered?		
Has the correct product been delivered?		
Have the correct codes been used on the invoice?		
Has the correct discount been applied?		

BPP
LEARNING
MEDIA

(b) Based on the amounts actually delivered to the customer, what should be the correct amounts of the invoice?

Net amount £	VAT amount £	Gross amount £

Task 4.6

Given below is a credit note and a goods returned note from a customer, Whitehill Superstores. Whitehill Superstores receives 20% trade discount on all orders.

Credit note

Southfield Electrical
Industrial Estate, Benham DR6 2FF
VAT Registration No. 569 5242 89

To: Whitehill Superstores   22 Oct 20XX

Credit note No. 08669

Purchase order 40102

	£
3 product 4770 @ £220 each	660.00
VAT @ 20%	132.00
Total	792.00

Reason: ordered in error

Goods returned note

Whitehill Superstores
28 Whitehill Park
Benham DR6 5LM

To: Southfield Electrical   19 Oct 20XX

Goods returned note No. 56

Purchase order 40102

4 product 4770 @ £220 each less 20% trade discount

Reason: faulty goods

Identify any discrepancies on the credit note by drawing a line between each left hand box and then the appropriate right hand box.

| Reason for return |

| VAT rate |

| Trade discount |

| Quantity |

| Not shown on credit note |

| Incorrectly shown on credit note |

| Correctly shown on credit note |

Task 4.7

Southfield Electrical received a cheque for £516.10 from a credit customer, Hayworth Ltd, on 20 November 20XX. There was no document included with the cheque to show what transactions were included in the payment.

(a)   **Show what document the customer should have included with the cheque by circling one document name.**

Document names
Delivery note   Petty cash voucher   Purchase order   Remittance advice note

After contacting Hayworth Ltd, you identify that the payment covers the invoice shown below.

Invoice number	30227	
Date:	7 November 20XX	
To:	Hayworth Ltd	
		£
Goods value		448.00
VAT		89.60
Invoice total		537.60

4% prompt payment discount for payment received within 10 days of invoice date, otherwise 30 days net

(b)   **Using the picklist below, complete the following statement.**

The cheque from Hayworth Ltd for £516.10 has resulted in an [▼]

This is because Hayworth has taken the [▼] offered.

This should not have been taken as the cheque arrived [▼] after the invoice date.

In order to resolve the problem Southfield Electrical should [▼] from Hayworth Ltd for £ [   ] which will clear the outstanding balance.

Picklist:

13 days
14 days
less than 10 days
overpayment
prompt payment discount
request a credit note
request an invoice
request another cheque
trade discount
underpayment

Task 4.8

Southfield Electrical received a cheque for £709.48 from a credit customer, Harper & Sons, with a remittance advice stating the payment was for invoice **30256**, shown below. The cheque was received on 19 November 20XX.

Invoice number	30256	
Date:	12 November XX	
To:	Harper & Sons	
		£
Goods value		620.00
VAT		124.00
Invoice total		744.00

4% prompt payment discount for payment received within 10 days of invoice date, otherwise 30 days net

Using the picklist below, complete the following statement.

The cheque from Harper & Sons for £709.48 has resulted in an [underpayment ▼]

Harper & Sons paid within the time limit for the [prompt payment discount ▼] offered by Southfield Electrical.

However, they [incorrectly calculated ▼] the discount.

In order to resolve the problem Southfield Electrical should [request another cheque ▼] from Harper & Sons for £ [4.76] which will clear the outstanding balance.

Picklist:

correctly calculated
incorrectly calculated
overpayment
prompt payment discount
request a credit note
request an invoice
request another cheque
trade discount
underpayment

Task 4.9

On 21 December Sumberton Ltd delivered the following goods to a credit customer, Gringles Co.

Sumberton Ltd
Sumberton House
10 Main Road
Sawlow
SA7 5LD

Delivery note No. 6734527
21 December 20XX

Gringles Co   Customer account code: RL 637
Unit 18 Radley Estate
Sawlow
SA7 7VB

80 leather shoulder bags, product code L736B.

The list price of the goods was £100 per box of five bags plus VAT. Gringles Co is to be given a 15% bulk discount and a 4% discount if the invoice is paid within 10 days.

Complete the invoice below.

Sumberton Ltd
Sumberton House,
10 Main Road
Sawlow
SA7 5LD

VAT Registration No. 536 3723 77

Gringles Co   Customer account code: RL 637
Unit 18 Radley Estate
Sawlow
SA7 7VB

Date: 22 December 20XX

Invoice No: 12901
Delivery note number: 6734527

Quantity of goods	Product code	Total list price £	Net amount after bulk discount £	VAT £	Gross £

Task 4.10

The account shown below is in the receivables ledger of Sumberton Ltd. A remittance advice for an automated payment of £2,807 has now been received from this customer.

Meering Ltd

Date 20XX	Details	Amount £	Date 20XX	Details	Amount £
6 October	Sales invoice 12624	1,756	10 October	Sales returns credit note 501	78
11 November	Sales invoice 12711	2,918	17 November	Sales returns credit note 555	111
7 December	Sales invoice 12813	2,384	30 November	Bank	1,678

Which outstanding item has not been included in the payment of £2,807?

[▼]

Picklist:

Bank
Sales invoice 12624
Sales invoice 12711
Sales invoice 12813
Sales returns credit note 501
Sales returns credit note 555

Chapter 5 – Recording credit purchases

Task 5.1

Ken trades in exotic dress materials.

Complete the following statement:

When a supplier delivers materials to him he retains the supplier's delivery note and also prepares

| ▼ | once he has had a chance to inspect the quality of the items.

Picklist:

an invoice
a goods received note
a remittance advice

Task 5.2

Complete the following statement:

A code which will help Ken to classify the different types of material purchase when completing his analysed purchases daybook is:

	✓
A supplier code	
A product code	⟋

Task 5.3

Ken has been offered a prompt payment discount by one of his suppliers of '2% for payment within 10 days'. He receives an invoice dated 10 June on 12 June with a total of £239.20, excluding VAT. He wishes to take advantage of the discount.

(a) **By what date must the supplier receive the payment?**

| ▼ |

Picklist:

19 June

20 June

21 June

22 June

(b) **How much should Ken pay the supplier on that date?**

£ |

Task 5.4

You work for Newmans, a music shop, in the accounts department and one of your responsibilities is to organise the payments to suppliers. You have been off sick for the last week and a half and therefore it is urgent that you consider the invoices that are on your desk requiring payment.

Newmans' policy is to pay any invoices that are due each Friday. When a cheque is written on a Friday it does not then reach the supplier until Monday, ie three days later. If a prompt payment discount is offered by a supplier then this is taken if the discount will still be valid on the Monday. Otherwise the policy is to take the maximum amount of credit available.

Today's date is Friday 27 January 20XX. Thereafter, the following payment dates are 3 February, 10 February and 17 February. Remember that, as payments take three days to reach the supplier, any invoice dated earlier than 7 January with a 30-day period must be paid today, because if they are delayed until 3 February then the payments will not be received until 6 February, more than 30 days after they are due.

The invoices that are on your desk are scheduled below:

Invoice date	Supplier name	Terms	Total £	VAT £	Net £
5 Jan	Henson Press	30 days	336.00	56.00	280.00
8 Jan	GH Publications	30 days	136.80	22.80	114.00
12 Jan	Ely Instruments	20 days 2% discount otherwise 30 days	765.00	127.50	637.50
15 Jan	Hams Instruments	14 days 2.5% discount otherwise 30 days	372.00	62.00	310.00
19 Jan	CD Supplies	10 days 3% discount otherwise 30 days	138.72	23.12	115.60
22 Jan	Jester Press	10 days 3.5% discount otherwise 30 days	156.00	26.00	130.00
22 Jan	Henson Press	30 days	306.00	51.00	255.00

In the schedule given below show the date that each invoice should be paid and the amount for which the cheque should be written out.

Invoice date	Supplier name	Payment date	Amount of cheque £
5 Jan	Henson Press	▼	
8 Jan	GH Publications	▼	
12 Jan	Ely Instruments	▼	
15 Jan	Hams Instruments	▼	
19 Jan	CD Supplies	▼	
22 Jan	Jester Press	▼	
22 Jan	Henson Press	▼	

Picklist:

27 Jan
3 Feb
10 Feb
17 Feb

Task 5.5

Given below is a statement received by your organisation, Edgehill Designs, from one of its credit suppliers, P T Supplies, as at 31 January 20XX. You are instructed to pay all of the invoices less credit notes up to 10 January. Today's date is 7 February.

PT Supplies 149 Field Road, Darton, DF12 8GH

STATEMENT OF ACCOUNT

To: Edgehill Designs   31 January 20XX

Date 20XX	Invoice/credit note number	Details	Amount £
6 Jan	Inv 20671	Goods	107
8 Jan	Inv 20692	Goods	157
10 Jan	CN 04722	Goods returned	28
27 Jan	Inv 20718	Goods	120
30 Jan	CN 04786	Goods returned	16
6 Jan	Inv 20671	Goods	107

(a)   Complete the remittance advice below by:

- Selecting the date from the picklist in the first column

- Dragging and dropping the appropriate details and transaction amount below into the second column

You only need to enter the relevant invoices and credit notes. Leave blank any rows that are not needed.

Remittance advice

To: PT Supplies   From: Edgehill Designs

Date: 7 February 20XX

Date 20XX	Details and transaction amount £
▼	
▼	
▼	
▼	
▼	

Picklist:

6 Jan
8 Jan

10 Jan
27 Jan
30 Jan
7 Feb

Details and transaction amount (£):

Inv 20671 – £107	Inv 20692 – £157	CN 04722 – £28
Inv 20718 – £120	CN 04786 – £16	

(b) What is the total payment amount to accompany this remittance advice note?

£ _____

Task 5.6

On 12 July Whitehill Superstores ordered goods from Southfield Electrical who agreed a 10% trade discount and payment terms of 30 days net. The goods were delivered on 15 July and the invoice and goods received note are shown below.

Invoice

Southfield Electrical Industrial Estate Benham DR6 2FF VAT Registration No. 569 5242 89		
To: Whitehill Superstores Invoice No. 56389		15 Jun 20XX
		£
10 product code 9116 @ £24 each		240.00
VAT @ 20%		48.00
Total		288.00
Terms: Cash on delivery		

Goods received note

Whitehill Superstores
Goods received note GRN47422

15 July 20XX
Received from: Southfield Electrical
10 product code 9116 in good condition

(a) Refer to the information above and the goods received note and identify any discrepancies on the invoice by drawing a line between each left hand box and then the appropriate right hand box.

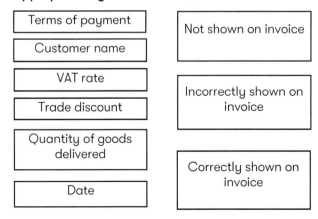

(b) **What will be the correct amounts on the invoice?**

Net amount £	VAT amount £	Gross amount £

Task 5.7

Given below is an invoice received by Dartmouth Supplies and the related purchase order.

Invoice

> Dan Industries
> Park Rise
> Fenbridge DR2 7AD
> VAT Registration No. 0621 3384 20
>
> To: Dartmouth Supplies   7 Oct 20XX
>
> Invoice No. 77412
>
> Delivery note 34816
> Purchase order 317428
>
> | | £ |
> |---|---|
> | 16 product D5345 Rocking chair @ £96.00 each | 1,536.00 |
> | Less trade discount @ 5% | 76.80 |
> | | 1,459.20 |
> | VAT @ 20% | 291.84 |
> | Total | 1,600.04 |
>
> Terms: 30 days net

Purchase order

> Dan Industries
> Order number 317428
>
> 20 Sept 20XX
>
> Please supply 16 product D4632 Rocking chair @ £96.00 each plus VAT
>
> Discount: 10% trade discount, as agreed

(a) Check the invoice and the purchase order and answer the following questions.

	Yes ✓	No ✓
Has the correct purchase price of the rocking chairs been charged?		
Has the correct discount been applied?		
Has the invoice been correctly cast?		
Has the correct product code been used on the invoice?		
Has VAT been charged at the correct rate?		

(b) What will be the correct amounts on the invoice?

Net amount £	VAT amount £	Gross amount £

Task 5.8

You work for Bailie Ltd. Shown below is a statement of account received from a credit supplier, Dazzle Ltd, and the supplier's account as shown in the payables ledger of Bailie Ltd.

Dazzle Ltd
21 Albert Street
Keeley
KE4 7AB

To: Bailie Ltd

5 Purley Road
Keeley
KE5 7LW

STATEMENT OF ACCOUNT

Date 20XX	Reference	Details	Debit £	Credit £	Balance £
1 July	8371	Goods	335		335
3 July	8412	Goods	420		755
7 July	8515	Goods	723		1,478
10 July	CN 3215	Goods returned		250	1,228
16 July		Cheque		485	743

BPP
LEARNING
MEDIA

Payables ledger – Dazzle Ltd

Date 20XX	Details	Amount £	Date 20XX	Details	Amount £
15 July	Bank – cheque	485	1 July	PDB 8371	335
15 July	Discount received	20	3 July	PDB 8412	420
			7 July	PDB 8515	723

(a)   Which item is missing from the statement of account from Dazzle Ltd?

	▼

Picklist:

Bank – cheque £485
Credit note 3215 £250
Discount received £20
Invoice 8371 £335
Invoice 8412 £420
Invoice 8515 £723

(b)   Which item is missing from the supplier account in Bailie Ltd's payables ledger?

	▼

Picklist:

Cheque £485
Credit note 3215 £250
Discount received £20
Invoice 8371 £335
Invoice 8412 £420
Invoice 8515 £723

(c)   Assuming any differences between the statement of account from Dazzle Ltd and the supplier account in Bailie Ltd's payables ledger are simply due to omission errors, what is the amount owing to Dazzle Ltd?

£	

Task 5.9

A supply of nails has been delivered to Acute Carpentry by Carbon Irons. The purchase order sent from Acute Carpentry, and the invoice from Carbon Irons, are shown below.

Acute Carpentry
Purchase Order No. 78639

To: Carbon Irons

Date: 16 June

Please supply 30 boxes 6 inch nails product code N1106
Purchase price: £20 per box, plus VAT
Discount: less 10% trade discount, as agreed.

Carbon Irons
Invoice No. 2318

Acute Carpentry

18 June

	£
30 .... boxes product code N1106 @ £25 each	750.00
VAT @ 20%	150.00
Total	900.00

Terms: 30 days net

Check the invoice against the purchase order and answer the following questions.

	Yes ✓	No ✓
Has the correct purchase price of the cardboard boxes been charged?		
Has the correct discount been applied?		

	Amount £
What would be the VAT amount charged if the invoice was correct?	
What would be the total amount charged if the invoice was correct?	

Task 5.10

Ken runs a business trading in exotic dress materials. He sends out cheques to suppliers on the last day of the month following the month of invoice. Below is an extract from Ken's payables ledger for his supplier, Mack Materials.

Mack Materials

Date 20XX	Details	Amount £	Date 20XX	Details	Amount £
31 May	Bank	890	1 May	Balance b/d	890
19 May	Purchases returns Credit note 43	31	7 May	Purchases Invoice 901	760
			3 June	Purchases Invoice 963	189

(a) Complete the remittance advice note below. Leave any spare lines blank. Enter all amounts as positive values.

Ken's Exotics
1 Bath Street
Cembury, CE11 9SD
REMITTANCE ADVICE

To: Mack Materials   Date: 30 June 20XX

Please find attached our cheque in payment of the following amounts.

Invoice number	Credit note number	Amount £
▼	▼	
▼	▼	
▼	▼	
▼	▼	
Total amount paid		

Picklist:

Balance b/d
Bank
Credit note 43
Invoice 901
Invoice 903

(b) Which of the following statements is true?

	✓
The remittance advice note will be sent to the accounts department at Mack Materials to request that a cheque is raised.	
The remittance advice note will be sent to Mack Materials's bank to advise them of the amount being paid.	
The remittance advice note will be sent to the customer to advise them of the amount being paid.	
The remittance advice note will be sent to the supplier to advise them of the amount being paid.	

Task 5.11

Ken has received a statement from a supplier which shows that, as at the end of June 20XX, he owes the supplier £2,876. The payables ledger account for this supplier shows that at that date Ken only owed £1,290.

Which of the following items would explain the difference?

	✓
Ken has requested a credit note from the supplier for £1,586 which he has not yet received.	
Ken sent a cheque for £1,586 to the supplier on 30 June 20XX.	
Ken ordered some items from the supplier on 30 June for £1,586 but the goods have not yet been delivered and an invoice has not yet been raised.	

Task 5.12

A supply of suitcases has been delivered to Sumberton Ltd by Casaubon's. The purchase order sent from Sumberton Ltd, and the invoice from Casaubon's, are shown below.

Sumberton Ltd Sumberton House, 10 Main Road Sawlow SA7 5LD Purchase Order No. 7683247
To: Casaubon's Date: 17 December 20XX Please supply 15 small wheeled cabin cases, product code WCC625 Purchase price: £23 each, plus VAT Discount: less 15% trade discount, as agreed.

Casaubon's 80 Eliot Street, Sawlow SA9 4AC VAT Registration No. 983 3933 83 Invoice No. 782736	
Sumberton Ltd Sumberton House, 10 Main Road Sawlow SA7 5LD 22 December 20XX	
	£
15 small wheeled cabin cases product code WCC625 @ £25 each	375.00
Less trade discount at 5%	18.75
Net amount	356.25
VAT @ 20%	71.25
Total	427.50
Terms: 30 days net	

Check the invoice against the purchase order and answer the following questions.

	Yes ✓	No ✓
Has the correct purchase price of the cabin cases been charged?		
Has the correct discount been applied?		

	Amount £
What would be the VAT amount charged if the invoice was correct?	
What would be the total amount charged if the invoice was correct?	

Task 5.13

Shown below is a statement of account received from a credit supplier, and the supplier's account as shown in the payables ledger of Sumberton Ltd.

Trinder and Papp
54 Vallais Road
Gosfirth
GO9 5VV

To: Sumberton Ltd
Sumberton House
10 Main Road
Sawlow
SA7 5LD

STATEMENT OF ACCOUNT

Date 20XX	Number	Details	Amount £	Balance £
20 October	10923	Invoice	2,109	2,109
4 November		Payment	–2,099	10
8 November	11004	Invoice	3,188	3,198
10 November	C536	Credit note	–156	3,042
26 November	11342	Invoice	2,185	5,227
28 November	11378	Invoice	1,244	6,471
30 November	C579	Credit note	–320	6,151

Trinder and Papp

Date 20XX	Details	Amount £	Date 20XX	Details	Amount £
4 Nov	Bank – BACS	2,099	20 Oct	Purchases	2,109
4 Nov	Discount	10	8 Nov	Purchases	3,188
10 Nov	Purchases returns	156	26 Nov	Purchases	2,185
			28 Nov	Purchases	1,244

(a) Which item is missing from the statement of account from Trinder and Papp?

[▼]

Picklist:

Credit note C536
Credit note C579
<u>Discount of £10</u>
Invoice 10923
Invoice 11004
Invoice 11342
Invoice 11378
Payment for £2,099

(b) Which item is missing from the supplier account in Sumberton Ltd's payables ledger?

[▼]

Picklist:

Credit note C536
Credit note C579
Discount of £10
Invoice 10923
Invoice 11004
Invoice 11342
Invoice 11378
Payment for £2,099

(c) Assuming any differences between the statement of account from Trinder and Papp and the supplier account in Sumberton Ltd's payables ledger are simply due to omission errors, what is the amount owing to Trinder and Papp?

£ [   ]

(d) Which of the following statements is true?

	✓
A credit note adds to the amount owed to the supplier	
A remittance advice note adds to the amount owed to the supplier	
A goods received note adds to the amount owed to the supplier	
An invoice adds to the amount owed to the supplier	

Chapter 6 – Double entry bookkeeping (part 1)

Task 6.1

Identify whether each of the following is an asset or a liability:

	Asset ✓	Liability ✓
A trade receivable	✓	
A car used in the business		✓
A loan from the bank		✓
A bank overdraft		✓
Cash in hand	✓	
VAT owed to HMRC		✓
A trade payable		✓
Inventory of raw materials	✓	

Task 6.2

Complete the following statements using the word 'debit' or 'credit' in each case:

An increase in an expense is a   Dr .

A decrease in a liability is a   Dr .

An increase in income is a   Cr .

An increase in an asset is a   Dr .

An increase in capital is a   Cr .

A decrease in an asset is a   Cr .

An increase in a liability is a   Cr .

A decrease in capital is a   Dr .

Task 6.3

(a) **Insert the two effects of each of these transactions in the space given below.**

(i) James paid £20,000 into a business bank account in order to start his business.

Effect 1	Effect 2
Decreas ▼	Increase in capital ▼

Picklist:

Decrease in capital
Decrease in cash
Decrease in liabilities
Increase in cash
Increase in capital
Increase in liabilities (trade payables)

(ii) He paid an initial rental of £2,500 by cheque for the shop that he is to trade from.

Effect 1	Effect 2
▼	▼

Picklist:

Decrease in capital
Decrease in cash
Increase in assets
Increase in cash
Increase in liabilities (trade payables)
Rent expense incurred

(iii) He purchased a van by cheque for £7,400.

Effect 1	Effect 2
▼	▼

Picklist:

Decrease in capital
Decrease in cash
Decrease in liabilities (trade payables)
Increase in assets
Increase in cash
Van expense incurred

(iv) He purchased £6,000 of goods for resale on credit.

Effect 1	Effect 2
▼	▼

Picklist:

Decrease in cash
Decrease in liabilities (trade payables)
Increase in assets (trade receivables)
Increase in cash
Increase in liabilities (trade payables)
Increase in purchases

(v)   He sold goods for £1,000 – the customer paid by cheque.

Effect 1	Effect 2
▼	▼

Picklist:

Decrease in cash
Decrease in purchases
Increase in assets (trade receivables)
✓ Increase in cash
Increase in liabilities (trade payables)
✓ Increase in sales

(vi)   He sold goods on credit for £4,800.

Effect 1	Effect 2
▼	▼

Picklist:

Decrease in cash
Decrease in purchases
Increase in assets (trade receivables)
Increase in cash
Increase in liabilities (trade payables)
Increase in sales

(vii) He paid shop assistants' wages by cheque totalling £2,100.

Effect 1	Effect 2
▼	▼

Picklist:

Decrease in cash
Decrease in liabilities (trade payables)
Increase in cash
Increase in drawings
Increase in purchases
Wages expenses incurred

(viii) He made further sales on credit for £3,900.

Effect 1	Effect 2
▼	▼

Picklist:

Decrease in cash
Decrease in purchases
Increase in assets (trade receivables)
Increase in cash
Increase in liabilities (trade payables)
Increase in sales

(ix)   He purchased a further £1,400 of goods for resale by cheque.

Effect 1	Effect 2
▼	▼

Picklist:

Decrease in cash
Decrease in liabilities (trade payables)
✗ Increase in assets (trade receivables)
Increase in cash
Increase in liabilities (trade payables)
✓ Increase in purchases

(x)   £3,700 was received from credit customers.

Effect 1	Effect 2
▼	▼

Picklist:

✓ Decrease in assets (trade receivables)
Decrease in liabilities (trade payables)
Decrease in sales
✗ Increase in assets (trade receivables)
Increase in cash
Increase in purchases

(xi)   He paid £3,300 to credit suppliers.

Effect 1	Effect 2
▼	▼

Picklist:

Decrease in assets (trade receivables)
Decrease in cash
Decrease in liabilities (trade payables)
Increase in assets (trade receivables)
Increase in cash
Increase in purchases

(xii)   He withdrew £800 from the business for his living expenses.

Effect 1	Effect 2
▼	▼

Picklist:

Decrease in cash
Decrease in liabilities (trade payables)
Increase in cash
Increase in drawings
Increase in purchases
Wages expenses incurred

48

(b) Enter James's transactions above in to his ledger accounts. You do not need to balance off the ledger accounts.

Bank

Details		£	Details		£
Capital (i)	▼	20,000	Rent (ii)	▼	
Sales (v)	▼		Wages (vii)	▼	
Trade Rec (x)	▼		Purchase (ix)	▼	
	▼		Bank (xi)	▼	
	▼		Drawing (xii)	▼	
	▼			▼	

Picklist:

Capital
Drawings
Payables ledger control
Purchases
Receivables ledger control
Rent
Sales
Van
Wages

Capital

Details		£	Details		£
	▼		Cash Bank (i)	▼	20,000
	▼			▼	

Picklist:

Bank
Capital
Drawings
Payables ledger control
Purchases
Receivables ledger control
Rent
Sales
Van
Wages

Rent

Details		£	Details		£
Bank ii	▼			▼	
	▼			▼	

Van

Details	£	Details	£
Purchase (iii) ▼		▼	
▼		▼	

Purchases

Details	£	Details	£
Bank (ix) ▼		Van (iii) ▼	
▼		Payable (iv) ▼	

Payables ledger control

Details	£	Details	£
Purchas (iv) ▼		▼	
Bak (xi) ▼		▼	

Picklist:

Bank
Capital
Drawings
Payables ledger control
Purchases
Receivables ledger control
Rent
Sales
Van
Wages

Sales

Details	£	Details	£
▼		Bank (v) ▼	
▼		Receivable le(vi) ▼	
▼		Receivable (viii) ▼	

Picklist:

Bank
Capital
Drawings
Payables ledger control
Purchases
Receivables ledger control
Rent
Sales
Van
Wages

Receivables ledger control

Details	£	Details	£
Sales (vi) ▼		Bank (x) ▼	
Sales (viii) ▼		▼	
▼		▼	

Picklist:

Bank
Capital
Drawings
Payables ledger control
Purchases
Receivables ledger control
Sales
Rent
Van
Wages

Wages

Details	£	Details	£
Bank (vii) ▼		▼	
▼		▼	
▼		▼	

Picklist:

Bank
Capital
Drawings
Payables ledger control
Purchases
Receivables ledger control
Rent
Sales
Van
Wages

Drawings

Details	£	Details	£
Bank (xii) ▼		▼	
▼		▼	
▼		▼	

Picklist:

Bank
Capital
Drawings
Payables ledger control
Purchases
Receivables ledger control
Rent
Sales
Van
Wages

Task 6.4

In this task, assume the business is NOT registered for VAT.

(a) **What is the double entry required for discounts allowed to customers?**

	Debit ✓	Credit ✓
Discounts allowed		✓
Receivables ledger control	✓	

(b) What is the double entry required for discounts received from suppliers?

	Debit ✓	Credit ✓
Discounts received	✓	
Payables ledger control		✓

(c) What is the double entry required for a purchase of goods for resale made on credit?

	Debit ✓	Credit ✓
Purchases		✓
Payables ledger control	✓	

(d) What is the double entry required for a sale made on credit?

	Debit ✓	Credit ✓
Sales		✓
Receivables ledger control	✓	

(e) What is the double entry required for a sale made for cash?

	Debit ✓	Credit ✓
Cash	✓	
Sales		✓

(f) What is the double entry required for cash received from a credit customer?

	Debit ✓	Credit ✓
Cash	✓	
Receivables ledger control		✓

(g) What is the double entry required for drawings made by the owner of a business?

	Debit ✓	Credit ✓
Drawings	✓	
Cash		✓

(h) What is the double entry required for wages paid in cash to employees?

	Debit ✓	Credit ✓
Wages	✓	
Cash		✓

BPP
LEARNING
MEDIA

Task 6.5

Indicate your answer by entering a tick (✓) in the relevant box.

Capital is also known as:

	✓
Asset	
Equity	✓
Expense	
Income	
Liability	

Chapter 7 – Double entry bookkeeping (part 2)

Task 7.1

The following account is in the receivables ledger of Smith & Co at the close of day on 31 May.

(a)   Insert the balance carried down together with date and details.
(b)   Insert the totals.
(c)   Insert the balance brought down together with date and details.

TN Designs

Date 20XX	Details	Amount £	Date 20XX	Details	Amount £
1 May	Balance b/f	2,643	8 May	Bank	1,473
11 May	Invoice 27491	1,804	24 May	Credit note 381	265
18 May	Invoice 27513	1,088			
▼	▼		▼	▼	
	Total			Total	
▼	▼		▼	▼	

Picklist:

31 May
1 June
Balance b/d
Balance c/d
Smith & Co
TN Designs

Task 7.2

The following account is in the payables ledger of Smith & Co at the close of day on 30 September.

(a)   Insert the balance carried down together with date and details.
(b)   Insert the totals.
(c)   Insert the balance brought down together with date and details.

Harold & Partners

Date 20XX	Details	Amount £	Date 20XX	Details	Amount £
7 Sept	Bank	635	1 Sept	Balance b/f	1,367
7 Sept	Discount	33	5 Sept	Invoice 27465	998
30 Sept	Credit note 364	106	12 Sept	Invoice 27499	478
▼	▼		▼	▼	
	Total			Total	
▼	▼		▼	▼	

Task 7.3

A payment by cheque is made to a supplier for £367.48.

What is the double entry for this transaction?

Account name		Debit £	Credit £
Bank	▼		✓
Payable ledger	▼	✓	

Picklist:

Bank
Payables ledger control
Purchases
Receivables ledger control
Sales

Task 7.4

For each of the following, indicate whether they are capital or revenue transactions:

	Capital ✓	Revenue ✓
Purchase of a new computer paid for by cheque		✓
Purchase of printer paper by cheque		✓
Purchase of a new business car on credit	✓	
Payment of road tax on a new business car		✓
Payment of rent for the business premises	✓	✓

Task 7.5

The following three accounts are in the general ledger at the close of day on 31 October.

Complete the accounts below by:

- Inserting the balance carried down together with date and details.
- Inserting the totals.
- Inserting the balance brought down together with date and details.

(a) **Payables ledger control**

Date	Details	Amount £	Date	Details	Amount £
31 Oct	Purchases returns	4,467	1 Oct	Balance b/f	41,204
31 Oct	Bank	36,409	31 Oct	Purchases	52,390
31 Oct	Discounts received	125			
▼	▼		▼	▼	
	Total			Total	
▼	▼		▼	▼	

Picklist:

31 Oct
1 Nov
Balance b/d
Balance c/d
Payables ledger control
Petty cash
VAT

(b) **Petty cash**

Date	Details	Amount £	Date	Details	Amount £
1 Oct	Balance b/f	200.00	31 Oct	Expenses	183.25
31 Oct	Bank	183.25			
▼	▼		▼	▼	
	Total			Total	
▼	▼		▼	▼	

Picklist:

31 Oct
1 Nov
Balance b/d
Balance c/d
Payables ledger control
Petty cash
VAT

(c) **VAT**

Date	Details	£	Date	Details	£
31 Oct	Sales returns	40.00	1 Oct	Balance b/f	183.25
31 Oct	Purchases	1,900.00	31 Oct	Purchases returns	62.00
			31 Oct	Sales	3,250.00
▼	▼		▼	▼	
	Total			Total	
▼	▼		▼	▼	

Picklist:

31 Oct
1 Nov
Balance b/d
Balance c/d
Payables ledger control
Petty cash
VAT

Task 7.6

For each of the following, indicate whether they are capital or revenue transactions:

	Capital ✓	Revenue ✓
Purchase of goods for resale on credit from a supplier		✓
Receipt of proceeds from sale of car used in the business	✓	
Payment of drawings to the business owner	✓	
Acquisition of new machine for use over five years	✓	
Payment by a cash customer for goods		✓

Task 7.7

The following two accounts are in the general ledger at the close of day on 30 November.

Complete the accounts below by:

* Inserting the balance carried down together with date and details;
* Inserting the totals; and
* Inserting the balance brought down together with date and details.

(a) **Purchases**

Date 20XX	Details	Amount £		Date 20XX	Details		Amount £
01 Nov	Balance b/f	140,389				▼	
15 Nov	Payables ledger control	14,388				▼	
30 Nov	Payables ledger control	52,389				▼	
▼		▼		30 Nov ▼	Bal c/d	▼	
	Total				Total		
1st Dec ▼		▼			▼	▼	

Picklist:

30 Nov
1 Dec
Balance b/d
Balance c/d
Bank
Payables ledger control
Purchases
Receivables ledger control

(b) **Bank interest received**

Date 20XX	Details		Amount £	Date 20XX	Details		Amount £
		▼		01 Nov	Balance b/f		32
		▼		15 Nov	Bank		14
		▼		30 Nov	Bank		22
▼		▼		▼		▼	
	Total				Total		
▼		▼		▼		▼	

Picklist:

30 Nov
1 Dec
Balance b/d
Balance c/d
Bank
Bank interest received
Payables ledger control
Receivables ledger control

Task 7.8

It is important to understand the difference between capital expenditure, revenue expenditure, capital income and revenue income.

Select one option in each instance below to show whether the item will be capital expenditure, revenue expenditure, capital income or revenue income.

Item	Capital expenditure ✓	Revenue expenditure ✓	Capital income ✓	Revenue income ✓
Purchase of airline tickets for business travel		✓		
Proceeds from sale of machinery			✓	
Sale of goods to a customer for cash				✓
Receipt of interest on the business's savings account from the bank				✓
Purchase of a shop building	✓			
Petty cash payment for stationery		✓		

Task 7.9

For each of the items below, identify an example from the picklist provided.

Item	Example
Asset	Trade Receivab ▼
Liability	Bank overdraft ▼
Capital transaction	Drawing ▼

Picklist:

Bank overdraft
Drawings
Trade receivables

Chapter 8 – Maintaining the cash book

Task 8.1

There are four payments to be entered in the credit side of Natural Production's cash book during one week.

Cash purchases listing

Suppliers paid in cash	Net £	VAT £	Gross £
Mendip plc	115	23	138

Trade payables listing

Credit suppliers paid by cheque	Amount paid £
W J Jones	521
Trenter Ltd	358
Packing Supplies	754

(a) Enter the details from the cash purchases listing and the trade payables listing into the credit side of the cash book shown below and total each column.

Details	Cash £	Bank £	VAT £	Cash purchases £	Trade payables £
Balance b/f		735			
▼					
▼					
▼					
▼					
Total					

Picklist:

Bank
Cash
Cash purchases
Mendip plc
Packing Supplies
Trade payables
Trenter Ltd
VAT
W J Jones

The debit side of the cash book shows the cash balance brought forward at the beginning of the week was £200 and a further £319 has been received during the week.

(b) Using your answer to (a) above, calculate the cash balance.

£ _____

The debit side of the cash book shows the total amount of money banked during the week was £560.

(c) Using your answer to (a) above, calculate the bank balance. If your calculations show that the bank account is overdrawn, your answer should start with a minus sign, for example −123.

£ _____

(d) Is the balance at bank calculated in (c) above a debit or a credit balance?

	✓
Debit	
Credit	

Task 8.2

Given below are the cheque stubs for the two payments made by Newmans on 27 January.

You have also looked at the standing order and direct debit instruction file and noted that there is a standing order due to be paid to the local council for business rates of £255 on the 27th of each month, and a direct debit for rent of £500 also due on 27th of the month.

Cheque book stubs

Henson Press
(Payables ledger account HEN006)
£329
000168

Ely Instruments
(Payables ledger account ELY003)
£736
000169

Make the necessary entries in the cash book and total each column.

Cash book – credit side

Details	Cash £	Bank £	VAT £	Trade payables £	Cash purchases £	Rent & rates £
▼						
▼						
▼						
▼						
Total						

Picklist:

Cash purchases
Ely Instruments
Henson Press
Newmans
Rates
Rent
Trade payables

Task 8.3

The two amounts shown below have been received from customers and are ready to be entered in the cash book.

<table>
<tr>
<td>
Receipt 56

11 July 20XX

Cheque for £500 and cash £334 received from Hoppers Ltd plc for goods supplied today – £834 including VAT.
</td>
<td>
Body Perfect

Remittance advice

13 July 20XX

An amount of £542 will be transferred to your bank account today by BACS, in full settlement of our May account.
</td>
</tr>
</table>

Make the necessary entries in the cash book and total each column.

Cash book – debit side

Details	Cash £	Bank £	VAT £	Trade receivables £	Cash sales £
Balance b/f	120	1,520			
▼					
▼					
Totals					

Picklist:

Bank
Body Perfect
Cash
Hoppers Ltd
Trade receivables
VAT

Task 8.4

The two amounts shown below have been received from customers and are ready to be entered in the cash book.

<table>
<tr>
<td>
Receipt 56

14 Oct 20XX

Cash £210 received from Howsham Ltd plc for goods supplied today – £210 including VAT.
</td>
<td>
Esporta Leisure

Remittance advice

14 Oct 20XX

Please find enclosed a cheque for £958 in full settlement of invoice 2457.
</td>
</tr>
</table>

Make the necessary entries in the cash book and total each column.

Cash book – debit side

Details	Cash £	Bank £	VAT £	Trade receivables £	Cash sales £
Balance b/f	56	1,805			
▼					
▼					
Totals					

Picklist:

Bank
Cash
Esporta Leisure
Howsham Ltd
Trade receivables
VAT

Task 8.5

There are five payments to be entered in Canlan Ltd's cash book.

Receipts from suppliers for Canlan Ltd's cash purchases

Supplier: Dubai Dreams		Supplier: Walter Enterprises		Supplier: Sinead Reilly
Received cash with thanks for goods bought.		Received cash with thanks for goods bought.		Received cash with thanks for goods bought.

Supplier: Dubai Dreams

Received cash with thanks for goods bought.

	£
Net	270
VAT	54
Total	324

Supplier: Walter Enterprises

Received cash with thanks for goods bought.

	£
Net	190
VAT	38
Total	228

Supplier: Sinead Reilly

Received cash with thanks for goods bought.

Net   £56
(No VAT)

Stubs from Canlan Ltd's cheque book

Payee: Sumatra Trading
(Payables ledger account PL026)

£7,265

Cheque number 093673

Payee: SHSK Co

For stationery
(Canlan Ltd has no credit account with this supplier)

£378 including VAT

Cheque number 093674

(a) Enter the details of the three receipts from suppliers and two cheque book stubs into the credit side of the cash book shown below. Total each column.

Cash book – credit side

Details	Cash £	Bank £	VAT £	Trade payables £	Cash purchases £	Stationery £
Balance b/f		236				
Dubai Dreams						
Walter Enterprises						
Sinead Reilly						
Sumatra Trading						
SHSK Co						
Total						

(b) There are two cheques from credit customers to be entered in the cash book:

Park Farm Stores   £2,576

Tristram Pale Ltd   £4,233

Enter these details into the debit side of the cash book and total each column.

Cash book – debit side

Details	Cash £	Bank £	VAT £	Trade receivables £
Balance b/f	1,228			
Park Farm Stores				
Tristram Pale Ltd				
Total				

(c) Using your answers to (a) and (b) above, calculate the cash balance.

£ [   ]

(d) Using your answers to (a) and (b) above, calculate the bank balance.

£ [   ]

(e) Is the bank balance calculated in (d) above a debit or credit balance?

	✓
Debit	
Credit	

Task 8.6

There are five payments to be entered in Kitchen Kuts's cash book.

Receipts

Received cash with thanks for goods bought
 	
From Kitchen Kuts, a customer without a credit account.
 	
          £
Net   200
VAT   40
Total   240
 	
B Smithson Ltd
	Received cash with thanks for goods bought.
	
	From Kitchen Kuts, a customer without a credit account.
	
	          £
	Net 160
	VAT 32
	Total 192
	
	H Hamnet
		Received cash with thanks for goods bought.
		
		From Kitchen Kuts, a customer without a credit account.
		
		Net £320
		(No VAT)
		
		Renee Reid

Cheque book stubs

Tenon Ltd (Payables ledger account TEN006) £3,600 000168	Vernon Motor Repairs (We have no credit account with this supplier) £48 including VAT 000169

(a) Enter the details from the three receipts and two cheque book stubs into the credit side of the cash book shown below and total each column.

Cash book – credit side

Details	Cash £	Bank £	VAT £	Trade payables £	Cash purchases £	Motor expenses £
Balance b/f		16,942				
B Smithson Ltd	240		40		200	
H Hamnet	192		32		160	
Renee Reid	320				320	
Tenon Ltd		3600		3600		
Vernon Motor Repairs	48		9.6			38.4
Total	800	20,542	81.6	3600	680	38 4

There are two cheques from credit customers to be entered in Kitchen Kuts' cash book:

G Brownlow   £749
S Barnett   £300

(b)   Enter the above details into the debit side of the cash book and total each column.

Cash book – debit side

Details	Cash £	Bank £	VAT £	Trade receivables £
Balance b/f	1,325			
G Brownlow		749		749
S Barnett		300		300
Total	1,325	1049		1049

(c)   Using your answers to (a) and (b) above, calculate the cash balance.

£ | 525

(d)   Using your answers to (a) and (b) above, calculate the bank balance.

£ | −19,493

(e)   Will the bank balance calculated in (d) above be a debit or credit balance?

	✓
Debit	
Credit	✓

Task 8.7

Shown below are the debit and credit sides of Halliday Ltd's cash book.

You are required to balance off Halliday Ltd's cash book.

Cash book – debit side

Details	Cash £	Bank £	VAT £	Trade receivables £	Cash sales £
Balance b/f	55	1,300			
Whippet's	210		35		175
Ragdoll Ltd		958		958	
▼					
Totals	265	2,258			
Bal b/d ▼	265	1,165			

Picklist:
Balance b/d
Balance c/d
Halliday Ltd
Ragdoll Ltd
Whippet's

Cash book – credit side

Details	Cash £	Bank £	VAT £	Trade payables £	Cash purchases £
Hornsea Ltd		355		355	
Lyndon Plc		738		738	
Bal c/d ▼	265	1,165			
Totals	265	2258			
▼					

Picklist:
Balance b/d
Balance c/d
Halliday Ltd
Ragdoll Ltd
Whippet's

Task 8.8

There are three receipts to be entered in the debit side of the cash-book during one week.

Cash sales listing

Sale made for cash	Net £	VAT £	Gross £
Humber & Co	485	97	582

Trade receivables listing

Credit customers paying by cheque	Amount paid £
Ridgely Ltd	2,150
Watts Partners	978

(a) Enter the details from the cash sales listing and the trade receivables listing into the debit side of the cash-book shown below and total each column.

Cash book – debit side

Details	Cash £	Bank £	VAT £	Trade receivables £	Cash sales £
Balance b/f	159	844			
Humber & Co	582		97		485
Ridgely Ltd		2,150		2,150	
Watts Partners		978		978	
Total					

The credit side of the cash-book shows cash spent on cash purchases of £561 during the week.

(b) Using your answer to (a) above, calculate the cash balance.

£ | 180

The credit side of the cash-book shows the total amount of cheques sent during the week was £4,085.

(c) Using your answer to (a) above, calculate the bank balance. If your calculations show that the bank account is overdrawn, your answer should start with a minus sign, for example –123.

£ | –113

Chapter 9 – Double entry for sales and trade receivables

Task 9.1

The following credit transactions have been entered into the sales daybook as shown below. No entries have yet been made into the ledgers.

Sales daybook

Date 20XX	Customer	Invoice number	Customer code	Total £	VAT £	Net £
Dec	S Himms	00011	RL 18	900	150	750
Dec	G Pood	00012	RL 13	1,500	250	1,250
Dec	M Kitchell	00013	RL 04	456	76	380
Dec	B Crown	00014	RL 15	1,392	232	1,160
Totals				4,248	708	3,540

(a) What will be the entries in the receivables ledger?

Receivables ledger

Account name	Amount £	Debit ✓	Credit ✓
▼			
▼			
▼			
▼			

Picklist:

B Crown
G Pood
M Kitchell
Payables ledger control
Purchases
Purchases returns
Receivables ledger control
Sales
Sales returns
S Himms
VAT

(b) What will be the entries in the general ledger?

General ledger

Account name	Amount £	Debit ✓	Credit ✓
▼			
▼			
▼			

Picklist:

B Crown
G Pood
M Kitchell
Payables ledger control
Purchases
Purchases returns
Receivables ledger control
S Himms
Sales
Sales returns
VAT

Task 9.2

The following credit transactions have been entered into the sales daybook as shown below. No entries have yet been made into the ledgers.

Sales daybook

Date 20XX	Customer	Invoice number	Customer code	Total £	VAT £	Net £
Jan	H Simms	0001	RL 45	1,800	300	1,500
Jan	P Good	0002	RL 21	3,000	500	2,500
Jan	K Mitchell	0003	RL 30	912	152	760
Jan	C Brown	0004	RL 05	2,790	465	2,325
Totals				8,502	1,417	7,085

(a) Post these transactions to the general ledger accounts shown below.

GENERAL LEDGER

Receivables ledger control

Details	Amount £	Details	Amount £
▼		▼	
▼		▼	
▼		▼	

Picklist:

Bank
Cash
C Brown
H Simms
K Mitchell
Payables ledger control
P Good
Purchases
Receivables ledger control
Sales
VAT

BPP
LEARNING
MEDIA

Sales

Details	Amount £	Details	Amount £
▼		▼	
▼		▼	

Picklist:

Bank
Cash
C Brown
H Simms
K Mitchell
Payables ledger control
P Good
Purchases
Receivables ledger control
Sales
VAT

VAT

Details	Amount £	Details	Amount £
▼		▼	
▼		▼	

Picklist:

Bank
Cash
H Simms
K Mitchell
Receivables ledger control
Sales
VAT

(b) **Post the transactions with H Simms and K Mitchell to the relevant accounts in the receivables ledger.**

Receivables ledger

H Simms   RL 45

Details	Amount £	Details	Amount £
▼		▼	

Picklist:

Bank
Cash
H Simms
Invoice 0001
Receivables ledger control

K Mitchell   **RL 30**

Details	Amount £	Details	Amount £
▼		▼	

Picklist:

Bank
Cash
Invoice 0003
K Mitchell
Receivables ledger control

Task 9.3

The following credit transactions have been entered into Natural Production's sales daybook as shown below. No entries have yet been made into the ledgers.

Sales daybook

Date 20XX	Customer	Invoice number	Total £	VAT £	Net £
2 Jan	Hoppers Ltd	6237	656.40	109.40	547.00
5 Jan	Body Perfect	6238	744.00	124.00	620.00
		Totals	1,400.40	233.40	1,167.00

(a) What will be the entries in the receivables ledger?

Receivables ledger

Account name	Amount £	Debit ✓	Credit ✓
▼			
▼			

Picklist:

Body Perfect
Hoppers Ltd
Natural Productions
Purchases returns
Receivables ledger control
Sales
Sales returns
VAT

(b) What will be the entries in the general ledger?

General ledger

Account name	Amount £	Debit ✓	Credit ✓
▼			
▼			
▼			

Task 9.4

The following credit transactions have been entered into Natural Production's sales daybook as shown below. No entries have yet been made into the ledgers.

Sales daybook

Date 20XX	Customer	Invoice number	Total £	VAT £	Net £
21 Jan	Esporta Leisure	6239	415.20	69.20	346.00
25 Jan	Langans Beauty	6240	273.60	45.60	228.00
		Totals	688.80	114.80	574.00

(a) **Post the totals of the sales daybook to the general ledger accounts given.**

GENERAL LEDGER

Receivables ledger control

Details	Amount £	Details	Amount £
▼		▼	
▼		▼	
▼		▼	

Sales

Details		Amount £	Details		Amount £
	▼			▼	
	▼			▼	

Picklist:

Bank
Cash
Esporta Leisure
Langans Beauty
Payables ledger control
Purchases
Receivables ledger control
Sales
VAT

VAT

Details		Amount £	Details		Amount £
	▼			▼	
	▼			▼	

Picklist:

Bank
Cash
Esporta Leisure
Langans Beauty
Receivables ledger control
Sales
VAT

(b) **Post the individual entries to the receivables ledger.**

RECEIVABLES LEDGER

Langans Beauty

Details		Amount £	Details		Amount £
	▼			▼	

Picklist:

Bank
Cash
Invoice 6240
Langans Beauty
Receivables ledger control

BPP
LEARNING
MEDIA

Esporta Leisure

Details	Amount £	Details	Amount £
▼		▼	

Picklist:

Bank
Cash
Esporta Leisure
Invoice 6239
Sales daybook

Task 9.5

The following credit transactions have been entered into Short Furniture's sales daybook as shown below. No entries have yet been made into the ledgers.

Sales daybook

Customer	Invoice number	Customer code	Invoice total £	VAT £	Net £
Rocks Garden Suppliers	08663	RL 22	701.76	116.96	584.80
Eridge Nurseries	08664	RL 07	429.30	71.55	357.75
Abergaven GC	08665	RL 16	923.40	153.90	769.50
Rother Nurseries	08666	RL 13	756.00	126.00	630.00
		Totals	2,810.46	468.41	2,342.05

(a) What will be the entries in the receivables ledger?

Receivables ledger

Account name	Amount £	Debit ✓	Credit ✓
▼			
▼			
▼			
▼			

Picklist:

Abergaven GC
Eridge Nurseries
Purchases returns
Receivables ledger control
Rocks Garden Suppliers
Rother Nurseries
Sales
Sales returns
Short Furniture
VAT

(b) **What will be the entries in the general ledger?**

General ledger

Account name		Amount £	Debit ✓	Credit ✓
	▼			
	▼			
	▼			

Picklist:

Abergaven GC
Eridge Nurseries
Purchases returns
Receivables ledger control
Rocks Garden Suppliers
Rother Nurseries
Sales
Sales returns
Short Furniture
VAT

Task 9.6

During January, Natural Productions issued some credit notes as shown in the sales returns daybook below. No entries have yet been made into the ledgers.

Sales returns daybook

Date 20XX	Customer	Credit note number	Total £	VAT £	Net £
17 Jan	Hoppers Ltd	1476	82.44	13.74	68.70
23 Jan	Esporta Leisure	1477	107.04	17.84	89.20
30 Jan	Superior Products	1478	14.16	2.36	11.80
		Totals	203.64	33.94	169.70

(a) **What will be the entries in the receivables ledger?**

Receivables ledger

Account name		Amount £	Debit ✓	Credit ✓
	▼			
	▼			
	▼			

Picklist:

Esporta Leisure
Hoppers Ltd
Natural Productions
Payables ledger control
Purchases
Purchases returns
Receivables ledger control

Sales
Sales returns
Superior Products
VAT

(b) **What will be the entries in the general ledger?**

General ledger

Account name		Amount £	Debit ✓	Credit ✓
	▼			
	▼			
	▼			

Picklist:

Esporta Leisure
Hoppers Ltd
Natural Productions
Payables ledger control
Purchases
Purchases returns
Receivables ledger control
Sales
Sales returns
Superior Products
VAT

Task 9.7

Natural Productions discounts allowed daybook is shown below. No entries have yet been made into the ledgers.

Discounts allowed daybook

Date 20XX	Customer	Credit note number	Total £	VAT £	Net £
1 Feb	Hoppers Ltd	1501	36	6	30
25 Feb	Esporta Leisure	1502	72	12	60
		Totals	108	18	90

(a) **What will be the entries in the receivables ledger?**

Receivables ledger

Account name		Amount £	Debit ✓	Credit ✓
	▼			
	▼			

Picklist:

Discounts allowed
Discounts received
Esporta Leisure
Hoppers Ltd

Payables ledger control
Purchases
Purchases returns
Receivables ledger control
Sales
Sales returns
VAT

(b) **What will be the entries in the general ledger?**

General ledger

Account name	Amount £	Debit ✓	Credit ✓
▼			
▼			
▼			

Picklist:

Discounts allowed
Discounts received
Payables ledger control
Purchases
Purchases returns
Receivables ledger control
Sales
Sales returns
VAT

Task 9.8

You work for Short Furniture. A remittance advice and cheque for £1,112.17 has been received from Rother Nurseries which they state is in full settlement of the account at 31 January. The remittance advice and the customer's account in the receivables ledger is shown below.

Rother Nurseries

REMITTANCE ADVICE

To: Short Furniture   Date: 1 Feb 20XX

Please find attached our cheque for full settlement of our account as at
31 January 20XX

Invoice number	Credit note number	Amount £
08666		756.00
08674		114.78
	1470	(96.50)
08681		337.89
Total amount paid		£1,112.17

RECEIVABLES LEDGER

Rother Nurseries   RL 16

Date	Details	£	Date	Details	£
9 Jan	Invoice 08666	756.00	20 Jan	Credit note 1470	96.50
16 Jan	Invoice 08674	214.78			
24 Jan	Invoice 08681	337.89			
5 Feb	Invoice 08695	265.98			

(a)   Check the remittance advice against the customer's account in the receivables ledger and state whether the following statements are true or false.

	True ✓	False ✓
Rother Nurseries has fully settled their account at 31 January 20XX.		
Rother Nurseries should have included invoice 08695 with their payment in order to fully settle their account at 31 January.		
The remittance advice note has been correctly cast.		
The invoice amounts are included correctly on the remittance advice note.		

(b)   What amount should Rother Nurseries have paid to fully settle their account as at 31 January?

£ [   ]

Task 9.9

A remittance advice and cheque for £2,279.30 has been received from Abergaven Garden Centre which they state is in full settlement of the account at 9 February. The remittance advice and the customer's account in the receivables ledger is shown below.

Abergaven Garden Centre

REMITTANCE ADVICE

To: Short Furniture   Date: 9 Feb 20XX

Please find attached our cheque for full settlement of our account as at 31 January 20XX

Invoice number	Credit note number	Amount £
08665		923.40
08672		623.56
08685		316.58
08692		415.76
Total amount paid		£1,863.54

80

Abergaven Garden Centre   RL 17

Date	Details	£	Date	Details	£
7 Jan	Invoice 08665	923.40	13 Jan	Credit note 1471	32.50
13 Jan	Invoice 08672	623.56	2 Feb	Credit note 1476	110.23
26 Jan	Invoice 08685	316.58			
3 Feb	Invoice 08692	415.76			

(a) Check the remittance advice against the customer's account in the receivables ledger and state whether the following statements are true or false.

	True ✓	False ✓
Abergaven Garden Centre has included on the remittance advice note all relevant transactions up to 9 February.		
The remittance advice note has been correctly cast.		
The invoice amounts are included correctly on the remittance advice note.		

(b) What amount should Abergaven Garden Centre have paid to fully settle their account as at 9 February?

£ [   ]

Task 9.10

The cash book should be treated as part of the double entry bookkeeping system.

Shown below are the totals of Natural Productions's cash book – debit side, at the end of the week.

Cash book – debit side

Date	Details	Cash £	Bank £	VAT £	Cash sales £	Trade receivables £
		279.84	2,018.10	46.64	233.20	2,018.10

What will be the entries in the general ledger?

Account name	Amount £	Debit ✓	Credit ✓
▼			
▼			
▼			

BPP
LEARNING
MEDIA

Picklist:

Bank
Cash
Cash purchases
Cash sales
Payables ledger control
Receivables ledger control
VAT

Task 9.11

Natural Productions' cash book – debit side, is shown below. The cash book is not part of the general ledger.

Date	Details	Cash £	Bank £	VAT £	Cash sales £	Trade receivables £
23 Jan	Hoppers Ltd		553.96			553.96
23 Jan	Superior Products		116.70			116.70
24 Jan	Cash sales	131.16		21.86	109.30	
25 Jan	Esporta Leisure		367.20			367.20
27 Jan	Cash sales	88.56		14.76	73.80	
27 Jan	Body Perfect		706.64			706.64
27 Jan	Cash sales	60.12		10.02	50.10	
27 Jan	Langans Beauty		273.60			273.60
	Totals	279.84	2,018.10	46.64	233.20	2,018.10

(a) **Post the entries to the individual accounts in the receivables ledger shown below.**

RECEIVABLES LEDGER

Hoppers Ltd

Details	Amount £	Details	Amount £
Invoice 6237	656.40	Credit note 1476	82.44
▼		▼	

Picklist:

Bank
Cash sales
Hoppers Ltd
Natural Productions
Payables ledger control
Purchases
Receivables ledger control
Sales
Trade receivables
VAT

Body Perfect

Details	Amount £	Details	Amount £
Invoice 6238	744.00	▼	
▼			

Picklist:

Bank
Body Perfect
Cash sales
Natural Productions
Payables ledger control
Purchases
Receivables ledger control
Sales
Trade receivables
VAT

Esporta Leisure

Details	Amount £	Details	Amount £
Invoice 6239	415.20	Credit note 1477	107.04
▼		▼	

Picklist:

Bank
Cash sales
Esporta Leisure
Natural Productions
Payables ledger control
Purchases
Receivables ledger control
Sales
Trade receivables
VAT

Langans Beauty

Details	Amount £	Details	Amount £
Invoice 6240	273.60		
▼		▼	

Picklist:

Bank
Cash sales
Langans Beauty
Natural Productions
Payables ledger control
Purchases

Receivables ledger control
Sales
Trade receivables
VAT

Superior Products

Details	Amount £	Details	Amount £
Invoice 6242	265.20	Credit note 1478	14.16
▼		▼	

Picklist:

Bank
Cash sales
Natural Productions
Payables ledger control
Purchases
Receivables ledger control
Sales
Superior Products
Trade receivables
VAT

(b)   **Post the totals to the general ledger accounts shown below.**

GENERAL LEDGER

Cash

Details	Amount £	Details	Amount £
▼		▼	
▼		▼	

Picklist:

Bank
Body Perfect
Cash
Esporta Leisure
Hoppers Ltd
Langans Beauty
Receivables ledger control
Sales
Superior Products
VAT

Bank

Details	Amount £	Details	Amount £
▼		▼	
▼		▼	

Picklist:

Bank
Body Perfect
Cash
Esporta Leisure
Hoppers Ltd
Langans Beauty
Receivables ledger control
Sales
Superior Products
VAT

Receivables ledger control

Details	Amount £	Details	Amount £
Sales	3,438.00	Sales returns	169.70
VAT	687.60	VAT	33.94
▼		▼	
▼		▼	

Picklist:

Bank
Body Perfect
Cash
Esporta Leisure
Hoppers Ltd
Langans Beauty
Receivables ledger control
Sales
Superior Products
VAT

Sales

Details	Amount £	Details	Amount £
▼		Receivables ledger control	3,438.00
▼		▼	

Picklist:

Bank
Body Perfect
Cash
Esporta Leisure
Hoppers Ltd
Langans Beauty
Receivables ledger control
Sales
Superior Products
VAT

VAT

Details	Amount £	Details	Amount £
Receivables ledger control	33.94	Receivables ledger control	687.60
▼			▼	

Picklist:

Bank
Body Perfect
Cash
Esporta Leisure
Hoppers Ltd
Langans Beauty
Receivables ledger control
Sales
Superior Products
VAT

Task 9.12

The following transactions all took place on 30 June and have been entered in the debit side of the cash book as shown below. No entries have yet been made in the ledgers. The cash book should be treated as part of the double entry bookkeeping system.

Cash book – debit side

Date 20XX	Details	Cash £	Bank £	VAT £	Cash sales £	Trade receivables £
30 Jun	Henderson & Co		7,349			7,349
30 Jun	Cash sale	426		71	355	

(a) What will be the entry in the receivables ledger?

Receivables ledger

Account name	Amount £	Debit ✓	Credit ✓
▼ Henderson Co	7,349	✓	

Picklist:

Bank
Cash
Henderson & Co
Payables ledger control
Receivables ledger control
Sales
VAT

(b) What will be the three entries in the general ledger?

General ledger

Account name	Amount £	Debit ✓	Credit ✓
Cash ▼		✓	
VAT ▼			
Bak ▼			

Picklist:

Bank
Cash
Henderson & Co
Payables ledger control
Receivables ledger control
Sales
VAT

Task 9.13

You work in the accounts department of Southfield Electrical. The following are extracts from the daybooks relating to transactions in May 20XX with Alpha Services & Co together with a remittance advice note for a cheque payment received in May 20XX from the customer.

Sales daybook – extract

Date 20XX	Customer	Invoice number	Customer code	Total £	VAT £	Net £
7 May	Alpha Services	715	RL 10	5,190.00	865.00	4,325.00
17 May	Alpha Services	787	RL 10	10,020.00	1,670.00	8,350.00

Sales returns daybook – extract

Date 20XX	Customer	Credit note number	Customer code	Total £	VAT £	Net £
12 May	Alpha Services	551	RL 10	624.00	104.00	520.00

REMITTANCE ADVICE NOTE Alpha Services	Remittance advice note number 013278
Supplier:	Southfield Electrical
Account number (supplier code)	PL 821

Date	Transaction reference	Amount £
21/04/XX	Invoice 600	289.50
27/04/XX	Credit note 401	(35.87)
1/5/XX	Payment made – cheque enclosed	253.63

BPP
LEARNING
MEDIA

Enter the transactions from the daybooks and the remittance advice into the customer's account in the receivables ledger. You do not need to balance off the account.

RECEIVABLES LEDGER

Alpha Services   RL 10

Details	Amount £	Details		Amount £
Balance b/d	253.63		▼	
715 ▼	5,190	551 ▼		624
787 ▼	10,020	Bal ▼		253
551 ▼			▼	

Picklist:

Alpha Services
Bank
Cash sales
Credit note 551
Invoice 715
Invoice 787
Payables ledger control
Purchases
Receivables ledger control
Sales
Southfield Electrical
Trade receivables
VAT

Task 9.14

The following transactions all took place on 30 November and have been entered into the sales daybook as shown below. No entries have yet been made into the ledger system.

Sales daybook

Date 20XX	Details	Invoice number	Total £	VAT £	Net £
30 Nov	Gringles Co	12786	300	50	250
30 Nov	Lester plc	12787	1,308	218	1,090
30 Nov	Shrier Goods	12788	2,676	446	2,230
30 Nov	Abunda Bags	12789	1,992	332	1,660
		Totals	6,276	1,046	5,230

(a) What will be the entries in the receivables ledger?

Receivables ledger

Account name	Amount £	Debit ✓	Credit ✓
Gringles Co ▼	300	✓	
Lester plc ▼	1,308	✓	
Shrier Goods ▼	2,676	✓	
Abunda Bags ▼	1,992	✓	

Picklist:

Abunda Bags
Gringles Co
Lester plc
Payables ledger control
Purchases
Purchases returns
Receivables ledger control
Sales
Sales returns
Shrier Goods
VAT

(b) What will be the entries in the general ledger?

General ledger

Account name	Amount £	Debit ✓	Credit ✓
VAT ▼	1046		✓
Sales ▼	5,230		✓
Receivable Ledger ▼	6,276	✓	

Picklist:

Abunda Bags
Gringles Co
Lester plc
Payables ledger control
Purchases
Purchases returns
Receivables ledger control
Sales
Sales returns
Shrier Goods
VAT

Chapter 10 – Double entry for purchases and trade payables

Task 10.1

You have been given an extract from your organisation's purchases daybook in respect of credit transactions in June. No entries have yet been made in the ledgers.

(a) Complete and total the purchases daybook shown below.

Purchases daybook

Date 20XX	Details	Invoice number	Total £	VAT £	Net £
30 June	Seashell Ltd	8971			3,211.00
30 June	Opal & Co	05119	4,800.00		
		Totals			

(b) Using your answer from (a) above, record the transactions in the payables ledger.

Payables ledger

Account name	Amount £	Debit ✓	Credit ✓
▼			
▼			

Picklist:

Net
Opal & Co
Payables ledger control
Purchases
Purchases returns
Receivables ledger control
Sales
Sales returns
Seashell Ltd
Total
VAT

Task 10.2

These are the totals of the purchases daybook at the end of the month. The cash book should be treated as part of the double entry bookkeeping system.

Purchases daybook

Details	Total £	VAT £	Net £	Purchases £	Stationery £	Packaging £
Totals	4,148.40	691.40	3,457.00	2,711.00	314.00	432.00

(a) **What will be the entries in the general ledger?**

Account name		Amount £	Debit ✓	Credit ✓
	▼			
	▼			
	▼			
	▼			
	▼			

Picklist:

Packaging
Payables ledger control
Purchases
Purchases returns
Receivables ledger control
Sales
Sales returns
Stationery
VAT

One of the entries in the purchases daybook is for an invoice from W J Jones for £210 plus VAT.

(b) **What will be the entry in the payables ledger?**

Account name		Amount £	Debit ✓	Credit ✓
	▼			

Picklist:

Discounts allowed
Discounts received
Payables ledger control
Purchases
Purchases returns
Receivables ledger control
Sales
Sales returns
VAT
W J Jones

Task 10.3

Natural Productions' purchases daybook is shown below. The cash book should be treated as part of the double entry bookkeeping system.

Purchases daybook

Date	Supplier	Invoice number	Total £	VAT £	Net £	Purchases £	Packaging £
31 Jan	P J Phillips	03576	428.40	71.40	357.00	357.00	
31 Jan	Packing Supplies Ltd	28423	321.60	53.60	268.00		268.00
			750.00	125.00	625.00	357.00	268.00

(a) **Post the totals of the purchases daybook to the general ledger accounts given.**

GENERAL LEDGER

Payables ledger control

Details	Amount £	Details	Amount £
▼		▼	
▼		▼	
▼		▼	

Picklist:

Packaging
Packing Supplies Ltd
Payables ledger control
PJ Phillips
Purchases
Purchases returns
Receivables ledger control
Sales
Sales returns
VAT

VAT

Details	Amount £	Details	Amount £
▼		▼	
▼		▼	

Picklist:

Packing Supplies Ltd
Payables ledger control
PJ Phillips
Purchases
Purchases returns
Receivables ledger control

Sales
Sales returns
VAT

Purchases

Details		Amount £	Details		Amount £
▼			▼		
▼			▼		

Picklist:

Packing Supplies Ltd
Payables ledger control
PJ Phillips
Purchases
Purchases returns
Receivables ledger control
Sales
Sales returns
VAT

Packaging

Details		Amount £	Details		Amount £
▼			▼		
▼			▼		

Picklist:

Packing Supplies Ltd
Payables ledger control
PJ Phillips
Purchases
Purchases returns
Receivables ledger control
Sales
Sales returns
VAT

(b) **Post the individual entries to the payables ledger accounts given.**

PAYABLES LEDGER

PJ Phillips

Details		Amount £	Details		Amount £
▼			▼		

Picklist:

Invoice 03576
Invoice 28423
Packing Supplies Ltd
PJ Phillips
VAT

BPP LEARNING MEDIA

Packing Supplies Ltd

Details	Amount £	Details	Amount £
▼		▼	

Picklist:

Invoice 03576
Invoice 28423
Packing Supplies Ltd
PJ Phillips
VAT

Task 10.4

Given below is Short Furniture's purchases daybook as at 27 January. The cash book should be treated as part of the double entry bookkeeping system.

Purchases daybook

Date	Supplier	Invoice number	Supplier code	Total £	VAT £	Net £	Wood purchases £	Polish/ varnish purchases £	Other purchases £
27 Jan	Ephraim Supplies	09642	PL39	349.20	58.20	291.00	291.00		
27 Jan	Cavendish Woods	06932	PL14	846.12	141.02	705.10	705.10		
27 Jan	Calverley Bros	67671	PL03	174.72	29.12	145.60		145.60	
27 Jan	Culverden & Co	36004	PL23	68.88	11.48	57.40			57.40
			Totals	1,438.92	239.82	1,199.10	996.10	145.60	57.40

(a) What will be the entries in the general ledger?

General ledger

Account name	Amount £	Debit ✓	Credit ✓
▼			
▼			
▼			
▼			
▼			

Picklist:

Other purchases
Payables ledger control
Polish/varnish purchases
Purchases returns
Receivables ledger control

Sales
Sales returns
Stationery
VAT
Wood purchases

(b)   **What will be the entries in the payables ledger?**

Payables ledger

Account name	Amount £	Debit ✓	Credit ✓
▼			
▼			
▼			
▼			

Picklist:

Calverley Bros
Cavendish Woods
Culverden & Co
Discounts received
Ephraim Supplies
Other purchases
Payables ledger control
Polish/varnish purchases
Purchases daybook
Purchases returns
VAT
Wood purchases

Task 10.5

Shown below is Thimble's purchases returns daybook. The cash book should be treated as part of the double entry bookkeeping system.

Purchases returns daybook

Date	Supplier	Credit note number	Total £	VAT £	Net £	Purchases £	Stationery £
10 Mar	K Mates	0326	235.20	39.20	196.00	196.00	
16 Mar	R Jones	C55	134.40	22.40	112.00		112.00
30 Mar	X & Y Ltd	563	297.60	49.60	248.00	248.00	
		Totals	667.20	111.20	556.00	444.00	112.00

(a)   What will be the entries in the general ledger?

General ledger

Account name	Amount £	Debit ✓	Credit ✓
▼			
▼			
▼			
▼			

Picklist:

Packaging
Payables ledger control
Purchases
Purchases returns
Receivables ledger control
Sales
Sales returns
Stationery
VAT

(b)   What will be the entries in the payables ledger?

Payables ledger

Account name	Amount £	Debit ✓	Credit ✓
▼			
▼			
▼			

Picklist:

K Mates
Payables ledger control
Purchases
Purchases returns
Receivables ledger control
R Jones
Sales
Sales returns
VAT
X & Y Ltd

Task 10.6

Shown below is Norris Day's purchases returns daybook. The cash book should be treated as part of the double entry bookkeeping system.

Purchases returns daybook

Date	Supplier	Credit note number	Total £	VAT £	Net £	Purchases £	Stationery £
10 Jan	Phillips	04216	117.60	19.60	98.00	98.00	
16 Jan	Wallace	CN0643	67.20	11.20	56.00		56.00
30 Jan	Olivia Ltd	CN1102	148.80	24.80	124.00	124.00	
		Totals	333.60	55.60	278.00	222.00	56.00

(a) Post the totals of the purchases returns daybook to the general ledger accounts given.

GENERAL LEDGER

Payables ledger control

Details		Amount £	Details	Amount £	
	▼		Purchases	2,711.00	
	▼		Stationery	314.00	
	▼		Packaging	432.00	
	▼		VAT	691.40	
	▼			▼	
	▼			▼	

Picklist:
Payables ledger control
Purchases
Purchases returns
Receivables ledger control
Sales
Sales returns
Stationery
VAT

VAT

Details		Amount £	Details		Amount £
Payables ledger control		691.40		▼	
	▼			▼	

Picklist:

Payables ledger control
Purchases

Purchases returns
Receivables ledger control
Sales
Sales returns
Stationery
VAT

Purchases returns

Details	Amount £	Details	Amount £
▼		▼	
▼		▼	

Picklist:
Payables ledger control
Purchases
Purchases returns
Receivables ledger control
Sales
Sales returns
Stationery
VAT

Stationery

Details	Amount £	Details	Amount £
Payables ledger control	314.00	▼	
▼		▼	

Picklist:
Payables ledger control
Purchases
Purchases returns
Receivables ledger control
Sales
Sales returns
Stationery
VAT

(b) Post the individual entries to the payables ledger accounts also given below.

PAYABLES LEDGER

Phillips

Details	Amount £	Details	Amount £
▼		Invoice 0357	428.40
▼		Invoice 0358	495.60
▼		▼	

Picklist:

Credit note 04216
Credit note CN0643
Credit note CN1102
Phillips
VAT

Wallace

Details	Amount £	Details	Amount £
▼		Invoice I342	252.00
▼		Invoice I350	124.80
▼		▼	

Picklist:

Credit note 04216
Credit note CN0643
Credit note CN1102
VAT
Wallace

Olivia Ltd

Details	Amount £	Details	Amount £
▼		Invoice 55773	748.80
▼		▼	

Picklist:

Credit note 04216
Credit note CN0643
Credit note CN1102
Olivia Ltd
VAT

Task 10.7

You work for Mountain Ltd and one of your duties is to transfer data from the cash book to the ledgers. The cash book should be treated as part of the double entry bookkeeping system.

Most of the payments are to credit suppliers but there are some cash purchases of materials from small suppliers which include VAT. The cash book – credit side is shown below.

Cash book – credit side

Date	Details	Cash £	Bank £	VAT £	Cash purchases £	Trade payables £
23 Jan	Time Ltd		1,105.07			1,105.07
23 Jan	Cash purchase	108.00		18.00	90.00	
24 Jan	WFF Ltd		252.00			252.00
	Totals	108.00	1,357.07	18.00	90.00	1,357.07

(a)   What will be the entries in the general ledger?

Account name		Amount £	Debit ✓	Credit ✓
Time	▼			✓
Cash	▼			✓
WFF	▼			✓

Picklist:

Bank
Cash
Payables ledger control
Purchases
Purchases returns
Receivables ledger control
Sales
Sales returns
Trade payables
VAT

(b)   What will be the entries in the payables ledger?

Account name		Amount £	Debit ✓	Credit ✓
Payable ledger	▼	13.57		✓
VAT	▼	18		✓

Picklist:
Payables ledger control
Purchases
Purchases returns
Receivables ledger control
Sales
Sales returns
Time Ltd
VAT
WFF Ltd

Task 10.8

The following credit transactions all took place on 30 November and have been entered into the purchases daybook as shown below. No entries have yet been made in the ledgers. The cash book should be treated as part of the double entry bookkeeping system.

Purchases daybook

Date 20XX	Details	Invoice number	Total £	VAT @ 20% £	Net £
30 Nov	Frankie's Leatherware	0923	12,348	2,058	10,290
30 Nov	Casaubon's	C6478	3,924	654	3,270
		Totals	16,272	2,712	13,560

(a) What will be the entries in the payables ledger?

Payables ledger

Account name	Amount £	Debit ✓	Credit ✓
Frankie ▼	12,349		✓
Casaubon ▼	3 9 24		✓

Picklist:

Casaubon's
Frankie's Leatherware
Payables ledger control
Purchases
Purchases returns
Receivables ledger control
Sales
Sales returns
VAT

(b) What will be the entries in the general ledger?

General ledger

Account name	Amount £	Debit ✓	Credit ✓
Payable ledger ▼			✓
VAT ▼		✓	
Purchases ▼		✓	

Picklist:

Casaubon's
Frankie's Leatherware
Payables ledger control
Purchases
Purchases returns
Receivables ledger control

Sales
Sales returns
VAT

Task 10.9

Natural Productions' discounts received daybook is shown below. No entries have yet been made into the ledgers. The cash book should be treated as part of the double entry bookkeeping system.

Discounts received daybook

Date 20XX	Customer	Credit note number	Total £	VAT £	Net £
3 May	Trenter Ltd	1501	36	6	30
10 May	WJ Jones	1502	72	12	60
			108	18	90

(a) What will be the entries in the payables ledger?

Payables ledger

Account name		Amount £	Debit ✓	Credit ✓
Trenter	▼	36	✓	
WJ Jones	▼	72	✓	

Picklist:

Discounts allowed
Discounts received
Payables ledger control
Purchases
Purchases returns
Receivables ledger control
Sales
Sales returns
Trenter Ltd
VAT
WJ Jones

(b) What will be the entries in the general ledger?

General ledger

Account name		Amount £	Debit ✓	Credit ✓
Dis rec	▼			✓
Trenter	▼		✓	
WJ Jones	▼		✓	

Picklist:

Discounts allowed
Discounts received
Payables ledger control

Purchases
Purchases returns
Receivables ledger control
Sales
Sales returns
Trenter Ltd
VAT
WJ Jones

Task 10.10

The following transactions all took place on 30 November and have been entered in the credit side of the cash book as shown below. No entries have yet been made in the ledgers. The cash book should be treated as part of the double entry bookkeeping system.

Cash book – Credit side

Date 20XX	Details	Cash £	Bank £	VAT £	Cash purchases £	Trade payables £
30 Nov	Cash purchase	612		102	510	
30 Nov	Casaubon's		2,445			2,445

(a) What will be the entry in the payables ledger?

Payables ledger

Account name	Amount £	Debit ✓	Credit ✓
Casaubon's ▼	2,445		✓

Picklist:

Bank
Casaubon's
Discounts allowed
Discounts received
Payables ledger control
Purchases
Receivables ledger control
Sales
VAT

(b) What will be the three entries in the general ledger?

General ledger

Account name	Amount £	Debit ✓	Credit ✓
Cash Purchase ▼	510	✓	
Trade Payable ▼	2,445		✓
VAT ▼	102	✓	

Task 10.11

These are totals of the cash book at the end of the month. The cash book should be treated as part of the double entry bookkeeping system.

Cash book

Cash £	Bank £	VAT £	Trade receivables £	Cash sales £	Cash £	Bank £	VAT £	Trade payables £	Cash purchases £
550	6,893	59	4,368	295	550	6,893	–	2,492	–

What will be the entries in the general ledger?

Account name	Amount £	Debit ✓	Credit ✓
Payable ledger Control ▼	2,492		✓
VAT ▼	59	✓	
Cash Purchases Sale ▼	295	✓	
Receivable ledger Cout ▼	4,368	✓	

Picklist:

Bank
Cash
Cash purchases
Cash sales
Payables ledger control
Receivables ledger control
VAT

Chapter 11 – Accounting for petty cash

Task 11.1

Natural Productions has a petty cash system based on an imprest amount of £100 which is replenished weekly. On Friday 20 January the total of the vouchers in the petty cash box was £68.34.

How much cash is required to replenish the petty cash box?

£ 31·66

Task 11.2

Newmans, the music shop, has an imprest petty cash system based upon an imprest amount of £120.00. During the week ending 29 January the petty cash vouchers given below were presented, authorised and paid.

Petty cash voucher 0721	
	29 January 20XX
	£
Coffee	3.99
VAT is not applicable.	

Petty cash voucher 0722	
	29 January 20XX
	£
Taxi	8.94
VAT @ 20%	1.78
Total	10.72

(a) Complete the petty cash book by:

- Entering both transactions into the petty cash book below.

- Totalling the petty cash book and inserting the balance carried down at 29 January.

Petty cash book

Date 20XX	Details	Amount £	Date 20XX	Details	Amount £	VAT £	Travel £	Office expenses £
24 Jan	Balance b/f	120.00	27 Jan	Paper	7.12	1.18		5.94
			29 Jan	Coffee ▼	3.99			3.99
			29 Jan	Taxi ▼	10.72	1.78	8.91	8.71
			29 Jan	Bal c/d ▼	98.17			
	Total	120		Totals	120	2.96	8.91	9.93

Picklist:

Balance b/f
Balance c/d
Coffee
Office expenses
Taxi
Travel
VAT

BPP LEARNING MEDIA

(b) What will be the amount of cash withdrawn from the bank to restore the imprest level of £120.00?

£ | 9 8 · 1 7

Task 11.3

On the first day of every month cash is drawn from the bank to restore the petty cash imprest level to £75.

A summary of petty cash transactions during November is shown below:

Opening balance on 01 November	£22
Cash from bank on 01 November	£53
Expenditure during month	£16

(a) What will be the amount required to restore the imprest level on 01 December?

£ |

(b) Will the receipt from the bank on 01 December be a debit or credit entry in the petty cash book?

	✓
Debit	
Credit	

Task 11.4

Short Furniture has a monthly petty cash imprest system based upon an imprest amount of £150.00. The total amount of cash in the petty cash box at 31 January is £48.50.

The petty cash control account in the general ledger is given below. You are to balance the petty cash control account (this should be the same as the balance of cash in the petty cash box on 31 January).

Petty cash control

Date	Details	Amount £	Date	Details	Amount £
1 Jan	Balance b/f	150.00	31 Jan	Expenditure	101.50
▼	▼		31 Jan ▼	Bal c/d ▼	48 50
	Total	150		Total	150
1 Feb ▼	Bal b/d ▼	48 50	▼	▼	

Picklist:

31 Jan
1 Feb
Balance b/d
Balance c/d
Petty cash
VAT

Task 11.5

A business which is not registered for VAT has partially completed its petty cash book for November, as shown below.

(a) Complete the analysis columns for the four items purchased from petty cash.

(b) Total and balance the petty cash book, showing clearly the balance carried down at 30 November.

(c) Enter the balance brought down at 01 December, showing clearly the date, details, and amount. You do NOT need to restore the imprest amount.

Petty cash book

Debit side			Credit side					
Date	Details	Amount £	Date	Details	Total £	Stationery £	Postage £	Motor fuel £
1 Nov	Bal b/f	100	7 Nov	Postage stamps	20		20	
			15 Nov	Pens & pencils	18	18		
			22 Nov	Petrol	10			10
			30 Nov	Envelopes	15	15		
▼	▼		30 Nd ▼	Bal c/d ▼	37			
	Total	100		Total	100			
1st ▼	Bal b/d ▼	37	▼	▼				

Picklist:

30 Nov
1 Dec
Balance b/d
Balance c/d
Envelopes
Pens & pencils
Petrol
Postage stamps
VAT

Task 11.6

This is a summary of petty cash payments made by your business.

Post Office paid	£30.00 (no VAT)
Window cleaning paid	£25.60 plus VAT
MegaBus paid	£29.50 (no VAT)

(a) Enter the above transactions in the petty cash book.
(b) Total the petty cash book and show the balance carried down.

BPP
LEARNING
MEDIA

Petty cash book

Debit side		Credit side					
Details	Amount £	Details	Amount £	VAT £	Postage £	Travel £	Cleaning £
Bal b/f	175.00	Post of ▼	30		30		
		Window Cl ▼	30.72	5.12			25 60
		MegaBu ▼	29.50			29.50	
▼		Bal c/d ▼	84.78				
Total	175	Total	175				

Picklist:

Balance b/d
Balance c/d
Cleaning
MegaBus
Post Office
Postage
Travel
VAT
Window cleaning

Task 11.7

At the end of September the cash in the petty cash box was £9.76.

Complete the petty cash reimbursement document below to restore the imprest amount of £250.

Petty cash reimbursement		
Date: 30.09.20XX		
Amount required to restore the cash in the petty cash box	£	

Task 11.8

This is a summary of petty cash payments made by Kitchen Kuts.

Tom's Taxi paid	£18.00 (no VAT)
Post Office paid	£30.00 (no VAT)
SMP Stationery paid	£36.00 plus VAT

(a) Enter the above transactions, in the order in which they are shown, in the petty cash book below.

(b) Total the petty cash book and show the balance carried down.

Petty cash book

Debit side		Credit side					
Details	Amount £	Details	Amount £	VAT £	Postage £	Travel £	Stationery £
Bal b/f	150.00	Taxi ▼	18			18	
		Postoff ▼	30		30		
		Stat ▼	43.2	7.2			36
		Bal c/d ▼	58.8				
▼							
Total	150	Total	150				

Picklist:

Balance b/f
Balance c/d
Post Office
Postage
SMP Stationery
Stationery
Tom's Taxi
Travel
VAT

Task 11.9

At the end of the month the cash in the petty cash box was £3.45.

Complete the petty cash reimbursement document below to restore the imprest amount of £200.

Petty cash reimbursement		
Date: 31.07.20XX		
Amount required to restore the cash in the petty cash box	£	

Task 11.10

Ken trades in exotic dress materials. The following is the credit side of Ken's Petty Cash Book, which acts only as a book of prime entry.

Petty cash book – credit side

Details	Voucher number	Total £	VAT £	Office expenses £	Stationery £	Maintenance £
Tea, coffee and milk for office	1234	15.20		15.20		
Printer cartridge	1235	39.12	6.52		32.60	
Repair to fire extinguisher	1236	54.00	9.00			45.00
Totals		108.32	15.52	15.20	32.60	45.00

(a) What will be the five entries in the general ledger?

General ledger

Account name		Amount £	Debit ✓	Credit ✓
Petty Cash	▼	108.32		✓
office	▼	15.20	✓	
Station	▼	32.60	✓	
Menta	▼	45.00	✓	
VAT	▼	15.52	✓	

Picklist:

Bank
Cash
Maintenance
Office expenses
Petty cash
Purchases
Stationery
VAT

(b) Which entry would be omitted if Ken's Petty Cash Book operated as a general ledger account as well?

[▼]

Picklist:

Bank
Cash
Maintenance
Office expenses
Petty cash
Purchases
Stationery
VAT

Task 11.11

Benjamin operates a petty cash system whereby each week he withdraws £50 from the bank and puts it in the petty cash tin.

What type of system is this?

	✓
Imprest system	✓
Non-imprest system	

Task 11.12

Lucy operates a petty cash system whereby each Friday afternoon she puts £60 in to the petty cash tin. At the start of the week, Lucy had £75.23 in notes and coins in her petty cash tin.

This is a summary of petty cash payments made by Lucy during the week.

Taxi paid	£9.00 (no VAT)
Post Office paid	£15.00 (no VAT)
Suzie's Stationery paid	£36.00 plus VAT

On Friday afternoon, Lucy withdrew £60 from the bank and put it in the petty cash tin.

(a) **Enter the above transactions, in the order in which they are shown, in the petty cash book below.**

(b) **Total the petty cash book and show the balance carried down.**

Petty cash book

Debit side		Credit side					
Details	Amount £	Details	Amount £	VAT £	Postage £	Travel £	Stationery £
Balance b/f	75.23	Taxi ▼	9			9.00	
		Post off ▼	15		15 00		
		Statio ▼	43.2	7.2			36
▼		Bal c/d ▼	8.03				
Total	75 23	Total	75 23	7.2	15 00	9.00	36

Picklist:

Balance b/f
Balance c/d
Bank
Postage
Post Office
Stationery
Suzie's Stationery
Taxi
Travel
VAT

(c)   What is the balance in notes and coins in the petty cash tin on Friday after Lucy has added the £60 withdrawn from the bank?

£   68·03

Task 11.13

Sumberton Ltd maintains a petty cash-book as a book of prime entry and part of the double entry bookkeeping system. This is a summary of petty cash transactions in a week.

Stamps bought for £12.60, VAT not applicable.
Staplers bought for £18.90, including VAT.

(a)   Enter the above transactions into the partially completed petty cash-book below.
(b)   Total the petty cash-book and show the balance carried down.

Petty cash book

Details	Amount £	Details	Amount £	VAT £	Postage £	Stationery £
Balance b/f	175.00	Printer cartridges	17.40	2.90		14.50
		Stamps	12.60		12 60	17 60
		Staple.	18.90	3.78	15 12	15 12
		Bal c/d	126.1			
Total	175	Totals	175	6·68	12·60	27·82

Picklist:

Balance b/f
Balance c/d
Postage
Stamps
Staplers
Stationery
VAT

(c)   What will be the three accounts in the general ledger which will record the above transactions?

General ledger accounts	✓
Stamps	
Stationery	✓
Petty cash-book	
Petty cash control	
Postage	✓
Staplers	
VAT	✓

(d) **Complete the following statement by choosing one word.**

In order to top up the petty cash to the imprest amount, the petty cashier needs to prepare a:

	✓
Remittance advice note	
Cheque requisition form	✓
Petty cash claim	
Customer statement	

At the start of the next week cash was withdrawn from the bank to restore the imprest level of £175.

(e) **What is the amount of cash that would have been withdrawn from the bank to restore the imprest level?**

£	175

Answer Bank

Chapter 1

Task 1.1

	Cash transaction ✓	Credit transaction ✓
Purchase of goods for £200 payable by cash in one week's time		✓
Writing a cheque for the purchase of a new computer	✓	
Sale of goods to a customer where the invoice accompanies the goods		✓
Receipt of a cheque from a customer for goods purchased today	✓	
Purchase of goods where payment is due in three weeks' time		✓

Task 1.2

✓	
	A credit note
	A remittance advice
	A petty cash voucher
✓	An invoice

Task 1.3

✓	
	A credit note
	A goods received note
✓	A goods returned note
	An invoice

Task 1.4

(a)

	Document issued by Joe
Freddie asks Joe for a quote for 14 desks	Quotation
Joe delivers 14 desks to Freddie	Delivery note
Joe requests payment from Freddie	Invoice
Freddie pays his invoice and takes a prompt payment discount	Credit note

(b)

	Document issued by Freddie
Freddie places an order with Joe for 14 desks	Purchase order
Freddie accepts in to his warehouse delivery of 14 desks from Joe	Goods received note
Freddie returns one faulty desk to Joe	Goods returned note
Freddie pays his invoice	Remittance advice

Task 1.5

✓	An alphanumerical system
	A numerical system

Task 1.6

Customer	Customer code
Caledonian Ltd	Ca01
Jury's Brewery Ltd	Ju02

Task 1.7

The correct answer is: [Supplier code]

Task 1.8

(a)

Supplier code	PL244
General ledger code	GL001

(b)　　The correct answer is: | Product code |

Task 1.9

(a)

Supplier account code	VIN234
General ledger code	GL505

(b)　　The correct answer is: | To help trace relevant accounts quickly and easily |

Chapter 2

Task 2.1

Date 20XX	Details	Invoice number	Total £	VAT £	Net £
7 August	VXT Ltd	172	120	20	100

Working: VAT = 100 × 20%, Gross amount = 100 + 20 = 120

Task 2.2

Date 20XX	Details	Invoice number	Total £	VAT £	Net £
15 June	R Hart	365	648.00	108.00	540.00

BPP
LEARNING
MEDIA

Task 2.3

(a) – (b) Sales daybook

Customer	Invoice number	Total £	VAT £	Net £
Hoppers Ltd	6237	656.40	109.40	547.00
Body Perfect	6238	744.00	124.00	620.00
Esporta Leisure	6239	415.20	69.20	346.00
Langans Beauty	6240	273.60	45.60	228.00
Body Perfect	6241	657.60	109.60	548.00
Superior Products	6242	265.20	44.20	221.00
Esporta Leisure	6243	499.20	83.20	416.00
Hoppers Ltd	6244	285.60	47.60	238.00
Langans Beauty	6245	328.80	54.80	274.00
		4,125.60	687.60	3,438.00

Cross-cast check:

	£
Net	3,438.00
VAT	687.60
Total	4,125.60

Task 2.4

Daybook:	Sales returns daybook

Customer	Credit note number	Total £	VAT £	Net £
Hoppers Ltd	1476	82.44	13.74	68.70
Esporta Leisure	1477	107.04	17.84	89.20
Superior Products	1478	14.10	2.35	11.75

Task 2.5

Daybook:			Purchases daybook			

Date	Supplier	Invoice number	Total £	VAT £	Purchases (materials) £	Stationery £
4 Jan	P J Phillips	03576	428.40	71.40	357.00	
6 Jan	W J Jones	18435	252.00	42.00		210.00

Task 2.6

Daybook:			Purchases daybook				

Date	Supplier	Invoice number	Total £	VAT £	Purchases (materials) £	Stationery £	Packaging £
12 Jan	P J Phillips	03598	495.60	82.60	413.00		
16 Jan	Packing Supplies	28423	321.60	53.60			268.00
19 Jan	Trenter Ltd	18478	625.20	104.20	521.00		
20 Jan	O & P Ltd	84335	748.80	124.80	624.00		
24 Jan	Packing Supplies	28444	196.80	32.80			164.00
28 Jan	Trenter Ltd	18491	441.60	73.60	368.00		
31 Jan	W J Jones	43681	124.80	20.80		104.00	

Task 2.7

Daybook:			Purchases returns daybook				

Date	Supplier	Credit note number	Total £	VAT £	Purchases (materials) £	Stationery £	Packaging £
10 Jan	P J Phillips	04216	117.60	19.60	98.00		
16 Jan	W J Jones	CN 0643	67.20	11.20		56.00	

Task 2.8

Date	Customer	Credit note number	Customer code	Gross total £	VAT £	Net £
21 Sep	Whitehill Superstores	08650	RL 44	356.40	59.40	297.00
23 Sep	Dagwell Enterprises	08651	RL 15	244.80	40.80	204.00
	Totals			601.20	100.20	501.00

Task 2.9

Date	Supplier	Invoice number	Supplier code	Total £	VAT £	Net £	Wood purchases £	Polish/ varnish purchases £	Other purchases £
27 Jan	Ephraim Supplies	09642	PL39	349.20	58.20	291.00	291.00		
27 Jan	Cavendish Woods	06932	PL14	846.12	141.02	705.10	705.10		
27 Jan	Calverley Bros	67671	PL03	174.72	29.12	145.60		145.60	
27 Jan	Culverden & Co	36004	PL23	68.88	11.48	57.40			57.40
				1,438.92	239.82	1,199.10	996.10	145.60	57.40

Task 2.10

(a) – (b)

Sales returns daybook

Date 20XX	Details	Credit note number	Total £	VAT @ 20% £	Net £	Bags returns £	Suitcases returns £
30 Nov	Shrier Goods	562	624	104	520	520	
30 Nov	Gringles Co	563	408	68	340		340
30 Nov	Lester plc	564	1,068	178	890	890	
	Totals		2,100	350	1,750	1,410	340

Chapter 3

Task 3.1

✓	A trade discount
	A prompt payment discount
	A bulk discount

Task 3.2

	The Home Office
	The Treasury
	The Inland Revenue
✓	HM Revenue & Customs

Task 3.3

Goods total £	Trade discount (15% × price) £	Net total £
416.80	62.52	354.28
105.60	15.84	89.76
96.40	14.46	81.94
263.20	39.48	223.72
351.00	52.65	298.35

Task 3.4

Net total £	VAT (Net × 20%) £	Gross total £
258.90	51.78	310.68
316.80	63.36	380.16
82.60	16.52	99.12
152.70	30.54	183.24
451.30	90.26	541.56

ANSWERS

Task 3.5

Gross total £	VAT (Invoice total × 20/120) £	Net total £
145.20	24.20	121.00
66.90	11.15	55.75
246.60	41.10	205.50
35.40	5.90	29.50
125.40	20.90	104.50

Task 3.6

Invoice total £	VAT (Invoice total × 20/120) £	Net total £
252.66	42.11	210.55
169.20	28.20	141.00
48.60	8.10	40.50
104.28	17.38	86.90
60.48	10.08	50.40
822.60	137.10	685.50

Task 3.7

Customer	Gross invoice total £	Amount £
J Smith	258	250.26
Anchorage Ltd	312	302.64
VIP Ltd	84	81.48
Blue House Ltd	150	145.50

Tutorial note. Multiply the gross total by 97% to give the amount payable by each customer.

Task 3.8

	£
Net amount before discounts	7,000
Net amount after discounts	6,517
VAT	1,303.4
Total	7,820.4

Workings

	£
Net amount before discounts	200 × 35.00 = 7,000
Net amount after discounts:	
Trade discount	7,000 × 5% = 350
After trade discount	6,650
Bulk discount	6,650 × 2% = 133
Net amount after trade and bulk discounts	6,517
VAT @ 20%	6,517 × 20% = 1,303.4
Total	7,820.4

Task 3.9

(a)

£	1,382.40

Working 1,280 × 1.2 × 90% = 1,382.40

(b)

Amount	£
Net amount	128.00
VAT	25.60
Gross amount	153.60

Working

Discount: 1,280 × 1.2 × 10% = 153.60, VAT = 153.60/6 = 25.60, Net amount = 153.60 − 25.60 = 128.00

Task 3.10

Daybook:	Discounts allowed daybook

Date 20XX	Details	Credit note number	Total £	VAT £	Net £
15 Oct	Shipper Ltd	223	67.20	11.20	56.00

Tutorial note. The credit note should be recorded in Anchor Supplies Ltd's discounts allowed daybook as it is a discount allowed to a customer.

The name of the customer (Shipper Ltd) should be recorded in the 'details' column.

Task 3.11

Daybook:	Discounts received daybook

Date 20XX	Details	Credit note number	Total £	VAT £	Net £
10 Nov	Rent a Van Ltd	11	123.60	20.60	103.00

Tutorial note. The credit note should be recorded in Pop Ice Cream Ltd's discounts received daybook as it is a discount received from a supplier.

The name of the supplier (Rent a Van Ltd) should be recorded in the 'details' column.

Task 3.12

(a)   The correct answer is: £ | 2,304

Working Gross amount = ((£2,000 × 20%) + £2,000) = £2,400

Amount after discount = £2,400 × 96% = £2,304

(b)   The correct answer is: £ | 2,400   (£2,000 + £400)

Task 3.13

The correct answer is: Trade discount

Task 3.14

	True ✓	False ✓
The book of prime entry for discounts allowed is the petty cash book.		✓
Input tax is the VAT suffered on purchases.	✓	
A goods received note is a primary document for recording in the accounting records.		✓

ANSWERS

Chapter 4

Task 4.1

✓	
	A delivery note
✓	A price list
	A goods received note
	A statement of account

Task 4.2

✓	
	Analyse every invoice into a separate column of his analysed sales daybook
✓	Allocate one of two sales codes to each invoice and use this to write up the invoices in the analysed sales daybook
	Allocate invoice numbers on a randomised basis
	Use a different sequence of invoice numbers for each customer

Task 4.3

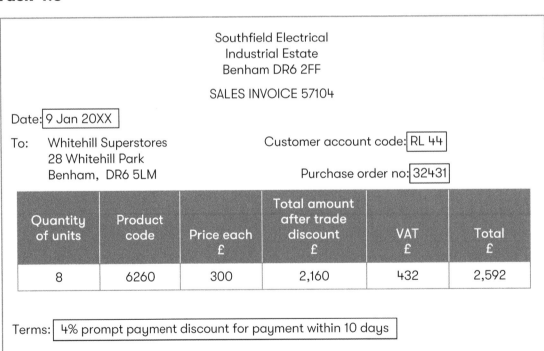

Southfield Electrical
Industrial Estate
Benham DR6 2FF

SALES INVOICE 57104

Date: 9 Jan 20XX

To: Whitehill Superstores
28 Whitehill Park
Benham, DR6 5LM

Customer account code: RL 44

Purchase order no: 32431

Quantity of units	Product code	Price each £	Total amount after trade discount £	VAT £	Total £
8	6260	300	2,160	432	2,592

Terms: 4% prompt payment discount for payment within 10 days

Tutorial note. The invoice is dated 9 Jan 20XX as the goods are delivered on this date.

BPP
LEARNING
MEDIA

Workings

	Calculation	£
Total list price	8 × 300	2,400
Trade discount	2,400 × 10%	240
Net amount	2,400 – 240	2,160
VAT	2,160 × 20%	432
Total	2,160 + 432	2,592

Task 4.4

Southfield Electrical
Industrial Estate
Benham DR6 2FF

SALES INVOICE 57105

Date: 19 May 20XX

To: Harper & Sons
      30 High Street
      Benham, DR6 4ST

Customer account code: RL 26

Purchase order no: 04367

Quantity of units	Product code	Price each £	Total amount after discounts £	VAT £	Total £
6	6370	260	1,407.9	281.58	1,689.48

Terms: 3% prompt payment discount for payment within 14 days

Tutorial note. The invoice is dated 19 May 20XX as this is the date the goods are delivered.

Workings

	Calculation	£
Total list price	6 × 260	1,560
Trade discount	1,560 × 5%	78
Net	1,560 – 78	1,482
Bulk discount	1,482 × 5%	74.1
Net after discounts	1,482 – 74.1	1,407.9
VAT	1,407.9 × 20%	281.58
Total	1,407.9 + 281.58	1,689.48

Task 4.5

(a)

Questions	Yes ✓	No ✓
Has the correct amount of goods been delivered?		✓
Has the correct product been delivered?	✓	
Have the correct codes been used on the invoice?		✓
Has the correct discount been applied?		✓

Tutorial note.

The invoice is for 15 toasters (as ordered) whereas the delivery note shows that only 12 were delivered. The correct product has been delivered, but the wrong product code has been used on the invoice (9046 instead of 9406), the purchase order number on the invoice is also incorrect, it should be 32202.

The customer was entitled to a 5% trade discount which has not been applied to the invoice. Additionally the invoice should state that the customer has been offered a 3% prompt payment discount.

(b)

Net amount £	VAT amount £	Gross amount £
171.00	34.20	205.20

Workings

	Calculation	£
Total list price	12 × 15	180.00
Trade discount	180 × 5%	9.00
Net	180 – 9	171.00
VAT	171 × 20%	34.20
Total	171.00 + 34.20	205.20

Task 4.6

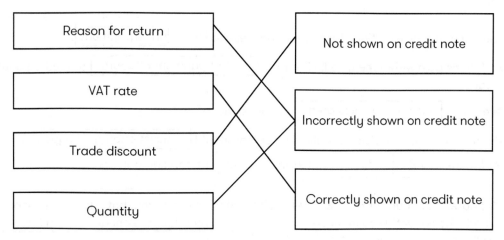

Reason for return	Not shown on credit note
VAT rate	Incorrectly shown on credit note
Trade discount	Correctly shown on credit note
Quantity	

Task 4.7

(a)

Document names

Delivery note   Petty cash voucher   Purchase order   (Remittance advice note)

(b)

The cheque from Hayworth Ltd for £516.10 has resulted in an [underpayment].

This is because Hayworth has taken the [prompt payment discount] offered.

This should not have been taken as the cheque arrived [13 days] after the invoice date.

In order to resolve the problem Southfield Electrical should [request another cheque] from Hayworth Ltd for [£ | 21.50] which will clear the outstanding balance.

Workings

Prompt payment discount: £537.60 × 4% = £21.50 has been deducted: £537.60 – £21.50 = £516.10. This should not have been taken as the cheque arrived 13 days after the invoice date.

Task 4.8

> The cheque from Harper & Sons for £709.48 has resulted in an underpayment.
>
> Harper & Sons paid within the time limit for the prompt payment discount offered by Southfield Electrical.
>
> However, they incorrectly calculated the discount.
>
> In order to resolve the problem Southfield Electrical should request another cheque from Harper & Sons for £ 4.76 which will clear the outstanding balance.

Tutorial note. A discount of £34.52 (£744 – £709.48) has been taken, but it has been incorrectly calculated. The correct discount is £744 × 4% = £29.76. Therefore the cheque should have been made out for £34.52 – £29.76 = £4.76.

Task 4.9

Sumberton Ltd
Sumberton House,
10 Main Road
Sawlow
SA7 5LD

VAT Registration No. 536 3723 77

Gringles Co
Unit 18 Radley Estate
Sawlow
SA7 7VB

Customer account code: RL 637

Date: 22 December 20XX

Invoice No: 12901
Delivery note number: 6734527

Quantity of goods	Product code	Total list price £	Net amount after bulk discount £	VAT £	Gross £
80	L736B	1,600	1,360	272	1,632

Tutorial note. Total list price: 80/5 × £100 = £1,600, Net amount after bulk discount = 1,600 × 85% = £1,360, VAT = 20% × £1,360 = £272, Gross = £1,360 + £272 = £1,632

Task 4.10

The correct answer is: Sales invoice 12813

Sales invoice 12624 £1,756 less Credit note 501 £78 = Bank payment £1,678.

Sales invoice 12711 £2,918 Less Credit note 555 £111 = £2,807.

The outstanding item that has not been included in the payment of £2,807 is Sales invoice 12813 £2,384.

Chapter 5

Task 5.1

When a supplier delivers materials to him he retains the supplier's delivery note and also prepares

| a goods received note | once he has had a chance to inspect the quality of the items.

Task 5.2

The correct answer is: | A product code |

Task 5.3

(a) The correct answer is: | 20 June |

(b) The correct answer is: | £ | 281.30 |

Workings

VAT: £239.20 × 20% = £47.84

Invoice total: £239.20 + £47.84 = £287.04

Discount: £287.04 × 2% = £5.74

Payment: £287.04 − £5.74 = £281.30

Task 5.4

Invoice date	Supplier name	Payment date	Workings	Amount of cheque £
5 Jan	Henson Press	27 Jan		336.00
8 Jan	GH Publications	3 Feb		136.80
12 Jan	Ely Instruments	27 Jan	765 × 98%	749.70
15 Jan	Hams Instruments	10 Feb		372.00
19 Jan	CD Supplies	10 Feb		138.72
22 Jan	Jester Press	27 Jan	156 × 96.5%	150.54
22 Jan	Henson Press	17 Feb		306.00

Task 5.5

(a)

<table>
<tr><td colspan="2">Remittance advice</td></tr>
<tr><td>To: PT Supplies</td><td>From: Edgehill Designs</td></tr>
<tr><td colspan="2">Date: 7 February 20XX</td></tr>
</table>

Date 20XX	Details and transaction amount £
6 Jan	Inv 20671 – £107
8 Jan	Inv 20692 – £157
10 Jan	CN 04722 – £28

(b)

£	236

Working

£107 + £157 – £28 = £236

Task 5.6

(a)

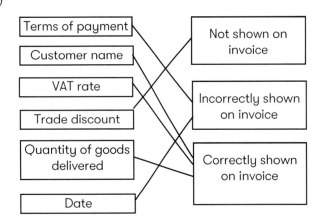

(b)

Net amount £	VAT amount £	Gross amount £
216.00	43.20	259.20

Working

	Calculation	£
Net before discount	10 × 24	240
Trade discount	240 × 10%	24
Net amount	240 – 24	216
VAT	216 × 20%	43.20
Total	216 + 43.2	259.20

Task 5.7

(a)

	Yes ✓	No ✓
Has the correct purchase price of the rocking chairs been charged?	✓	
Has the correct discount been applied?		✓
Has the invoice been correctly cast?		✓
Has the correct product code been used on the invoice?		✓
Has VAT been charged at the correct rate?	✓	

Tutorial note.

- Trade discount of 5% instead of 10% agreed has been deducted.

- The invoice has been incorrectly cast – the total of the net and VAT amounts should be £1,751.04.

- The product code on the invoice does not agree to that on the purchase order.

(b)

Net amount £	VAT amount £	Gross amount £
1,382.40	276.48	1,658.88

Working

	Calculation	£
Net before discount	16 × 96.00	1,536.00
Trade discount	1,536.00 × 10%	153.60
Net amount	1,536.00 – 153.60	1,382.40
VAT	1,382.40 × 20%	276.48
Total	1,382.40 + 276.48	1,658.88

ANSWERS

Task 5.8

(a) The correct answer is: | Discount received £20 |

(b) The correct answer is: | Credit note 3215 £250 |

(c) The correct answer is: | £ | 723 |

Working

£743 – £20 = £723

Task 5.9

	Yes ✓	No ✓
Has the correct purchase price of the cardboard boxes been charged?		✓
Has the correct discount been applied?		✓

	Amount £
What would be the VAT amount charged if the invoice was correct?	108.00
What would be the total amount charged if the invoice was correct?	648.00

Working

	Calculation	£
Net before discount	30 × 20	600
Trade discount	600 × 10%	60
Net amount	600 – 60	540
VAT	540 × 20%	108
Total	540 + 108	648

Task 5.10

(a)

Ken's Exotics
1 Bath Street

Cembury, CE11 9SD

REMITTANCE ADVICE

To: Mack Materials   Date: 30 June 20XX

Please find attached our cheque in payment of the following amounts.

Invoice number	Credit note number	Amount £
Invoice 901		760
	Credit note 43	31
Total amount paid		729

(b)

	✓
The remittance advice note will be sent to the accounts department at Mack Materials to request that a cheque is raised.	
The remittance advice note will be sent to Mack Materials's bank to advise them of the amount being paid.	
The remittance advice note will be sent to the customer to advise them of the amount being paid.	
The remittance advice note will be sent to the supplier to advise them of the amount being paid.	✓

Task 5.11

	✓
Ken has requested a credit note from the supplier for £1,586 which he has not yet received.	
Ken sent a cheque for £1,586 to the supplier on 30 June 20XX.	✓
Ken ordered some items from the supplier on 30 June for £1,586 but the goods have not yet been delivered and an invoice has not yet been raised.	

Task 5.12

	Yes ✓	No ✓
Has the correct purchase price of the cabin cases been charged?		✓
Has the correct discount been applied?		✓

	Amount £
What would be the VAT amount charged if the invoice was correct?	58.65
What would be the total amount charged if the invoice was correct?	351.90

Workings

VAT: (15 × £23) × 0.85 × 0.2 = £58.65

Total: (15 × £23 × 0.85) + £58.65 = £351.90

Task 5.13

(a) The correct answer is: | Discount of £10 |

(b) The correct answer is: | Credit note C579 |

(c) The correct answer is: | £ | 6,141 |

Working

(£6,151 – £10)

(d)

	✓
A credit note adds to the amount owed to the supplier	
A remittance advice note adds to the amount owed to the supplier	
A goods received note adds to the amount owed to the supplier	
An invoice adds to the amount owed to the supplier	✓

Chapter 6

Task 6.1

	Asset ✓	Liability ✓
A trade receivable	✓	
A car used in the business	✓	
A loan from the bank		✓
A bank overdraft		✓
Cash in hand	✓	
VAT owed to HMRC		✓
A trade payable		✓
Inventory of raw materials	✓	

Task 6.2

An increase in an expense is a	debit
A decrease in a liability is a	debit
An increase in income is a	credit
An increase in an asset is a	debit
An increase in capital is a	credit
A decrease in an asset is a	credit
An increase in a liability is a	credit
A decrease in capital is a	debit

Task 6.3

(a) (i) James paid £20,000 into a business bank account in order to start the business.

Effect 1	Effect 2
Increase in cash	Increase in capital

(ii) He paid an initial rental of £2,500 by cheque for the shop that he is to trade from.

Effect 1	Effect 2
Decrease in cash	Rent expense incurred

(iii)   He purchased a van by cheque for £7,400.

Effect 1	Effect 2
Decrease in cash	Increase in assets

(iv)   He purchased £6,000 of goods for resale on credit.

Effect 1	Effect 2
Increase in purchases	Increase in liabilities (trade payables)

(v)   He sold goods for £1,000 - the customer paid by cheque.

Effect 1	Effect 2
Increase in cash	Increase in sales

(vi)   He sold goods on credit for £4,800.

Effect 1	Effect 2
Increase in assets (trade receivables)	Increase in sales

(vii)   He paid shop assistants' wages by cheque totalling £2,100.

Effect 1	Effect 2
Decrease in cash	Wages expense incurred

(viii)   He made further sales on credit for £3,900.

Effect 1	Effect 2
Increase in assets (trade receivables)	Increase in sales

(ix)   He purchased a further £1,400 of goods for resale by cheque.

Effect 1	Effect 2
Decrease in cash	Increase in purchases

(x)   £3,700 was received from credit customers.

Effect 1	Effect 2
Increase in cash	Decrease in assets (trade receivables)

(xi)   He paid £3,300 to credit suppliers.

Effect 1	Effect 2
Decrease in cash	Decrease in liabilities (trade payables)

(xii)   He withdrew £800 from the business for his living expenses.

Effect 1	Effect 2
Decrease in cash	Increase in drawings

(b)

Bank

Details	£	Details	£
Capital (i)	20,000	Rent (ii)	2,500
Sales (v)	1,000	Van (iii)	7,400
Receivables ledger control (x)	3,700	Wages (vii)	2,100
		Purchases (ix)	1,400
		Payables ledger control (xi)	3,300
		Drawings (xii)	800

Capital

Details	£	Details	£
		Bank (i)	20,000

Rent

Details	£	Details	£
Bank (ii)	2,500		

Van

Details	£	Details	£
Bank (iii)	7,400		

Purchases

Details	£	Details	£
Payables ledger control (iv)	6,000		
Bank (ix)	1,400		

Payables ledger control

Details	£	Details	£
Bank (xi)	3,300	Purchases (iv)	6,000

Sales

Details	£	Details	£
		Bank (v)	1,000
		Receivables ledger control (vi)	4,800
		Receivables ledger control (viii)	3,900

Receivables ledger control

Details	£	Details	£
Sales (vi)	4,800	Bank (x)	3,700
Sales (viii)	3,900		

Wages

Details	£	Details	£
Bank (vii)	2,100		

Drawings

Details	£	Details	£
Bank (xii)	800		

Task 6.4

(a)

	Debit ✓	Credit ✓
Discounts allowed	✓	
Receivables ledger control		✓

(b)

	Debit ✓	Credit ✓
Discounts received		✓
Payables ledger control	✓	

(c)

	Debit ✓	Credit ✓
Purchases	✓	
Payables ledger control		✓

(d)

	Debit ✓	Credit ✓
Sales		✓
Receivables ledger control	✓	

(e)

	Debit ✓	Credit ✓
Cash	✓	
Sales		✓

(f)

	Debit ✓	Credit ✓
Cash	✓	
Receivables ledger control		✓

(g)

	Debit ✓	Credit ✓
Drawings	✓	
Cash		✓

(h)

	Debit ✓	Credit ✓
Wages	✓	
Cash		✓

Task 6.5

	✓
Asset	
Equity	✓
Expense	
Income	
Liability	

Chapter 7

Task 7.1

TN Designs

Date 20XX	Details	Amount £	Date 20XX	Details	Amount £
1 May	Balance b/f	2,643	8 May	Bank	1,473
11 May	Invoice 27491	1,804	24 May	Credit note 381	265
18 May	Invoice 27513	1,088			
			31 May	Balance c/d	3,797
	Total	5,535		Total	5,535
1 June	Balance b/d	3,797			

Task 7.2

Harold & Partners

Date 20XX	Details	Amount £	Date 20XX	Details	Amount £
7 Sept	Bank	635	1 Sept	Balance b/f	1,367
7 Sept	Discount	33	5 Sept	Invoice 27465	998
30 Sept	Credit note 364	106	12 Sept	Invoice 27499	478
30 Sept	Balance c/d	2,069			
	Total	2,843		Total	2,843
			1 Oct	Balance b/d	2,069

Task 7.3

Account name	Debit £	Credit £
Payables ledger control	367.48	
Bank		367.48

Task 7.4

	Capital ✓	Revenue ✓
Purchase of a new computer paid for by cheque	✓	
Purchase of printer paper by cheque		✓
Purchase of a new business car on credit	✓	
Payment of road tax on a new business car		✓
Payment of rent for the business premises		✓

Task 7.5

(a) **Payables ledger control**

Date	Details	Amount £	Date	Details	Amount £
31 Oct	Purchases returns	4,467	1 Oct	Balance b/f	41,204
31 Oct	Bank	36,409	31 Oct	Purchases	52,390
31 Oct	Discounts received	125			
31 Oct	Balance c/d	52,593			
	Total	93,594		Total	93,594
			1 Nov	Balance b/d	52,593

(b) **Petty cash**

Date	Details	Amount £	Date	Details	Amount £
1 Oct	Balance b/f	200.00	31 Oct	Expenses	183.25
31 Oct	Bank	183.25	31 Oct	Balance c/d	200.00
	Total	383.25		Total	383.25
1 Nov	Balance b/d	200.00			

(c) VAT

Date	Details	Amount £	Date	Details	Amount £
31 Oct	Sales returns	40.00	1 Oct	Balance b/f	183.25
31 Oct	Purchases	1,900.00	31 Oct	Purchases returns	62.00
31 Oct	Balance c/d	1,555.25	31 Oct	Sales	3,250.00
	Total	3,495.25		Total	3,495.25
			1 Nov	Balance b/d	1,555.25

Task 7.6

	Capital ✓	Revenue ✓
Purchase of goods for resale on credit from a supplier		✓
Receipt of proceeds from sale of car used in the business	✓	
Payment of drawings to the business owner	✓	
Acquisition of new machine for use over five years	✓	
Payment by a cash customer for goods		✓

Task 7.7

(a) Purchases

Date 20XX	Details	Amount £	Date 20XX	Details	Amount £
01 Nov	Balance b/f	140,389			
15 Nov	Payables ledger control	14,388			
30 Nov	Payables ledger control	52,389			
			30 Nov	Balance c/d	207,166
	Total	207,166		Total	207,166
1 Dec	Balance b/d	207,166			

(b) Bank interest received

Date 20XX	Details	Amount £	Date 20XX	Details	Amount £
			01 Nov	Balance b/f	32
			15 Nov	Bank	14
			30 Nov	Bank	22
30 Nov	Balance c/d	68			
	Total	68		Total	68
			1 Dec	Balance b/d	68

Task 7.8

Item	Capital expenditure ✓	Revenue expenditure ✓	Capital income ✓	Revenue income ✓
Purchase of airline tickets for business travel		✓		
Proceeds from sale of machinery			✓	
Sale of goods to a customer for cash				✓
Received interest on the business's savings account from the bank				✓
Purchase of a shop building	✓			
Petty cash payment for stationery		✓		

Task 7.9

Item	Example
Asset	Trade receivables
Liability	Bank overdraft
Capital transaction	Drawings

Chapter 8

Task 8.1

(a)

Details	Cash £	Bank £	VAT £	Cash purchases £	Trade payables £
Balance b/f		735			
Mendip plc	138		23	115	
W J Jones		521			521
Trenter Ltd		358			358
Packing Supplies		754			754
Totals	138	2,368	23	115	1,633

(b)   Cash balance is | £ | 381 |

Working £200 + £319 – £138

(c)   Bank balance is £1,808

Working £560 – £2,368

(d)

	✓
Debit	
Credit	✓

Task 8.2

Cash book – credit side

Details	Cash £	Bank £	VAT £	Trade payables £	Cash purchases £	Rent & rates £
Henson Press		329		329		
Ely Instruments		736		736		
Rates		255				255
Rent		500				500
Total		1,820		1,065		755

Task 8.3

Cash book – debit side

Details	Cash £	Bank £	VAT £	Trade receivables £	Cash sales £
Balance b/f	120	1,520			
Hoppers Ltd	334	500	139		695
Body Perfect		542		542	
Totals	454	2,562	139	542	695

Task 8.4

Cash book – debit side

Details	Cash £	Bank £	VAT £	Trade receivables £	Cash sales £
Balance b/f	56	1,805			
Howsham Ltd	210		35		175
Esporta Leisure		958		958	
Totals	266	2,763	35	958	175

Task 8.5

(a)   Cash book – credit side

Details	Cash £	Bank £	VAT £	Trade payables £	Cash purchases £	Stationery £
Balance b/f		236				
Dubai Dreams	324		54		270	
Walter Enterprises	228		38		190	
Sinead Reilly	56				56	
Sumatra Trading		7,265		7,265		
SHSK Co		378	63			315
Total	608	7,879	155	7,265	516	315

(b) **Cash book – debit side**

Details	Cash £	Bank £	VAT £	Trade receivables £
Balance b/f	1,228			
Park Farm Stores		2,576		2,576
Tristram Pale Ltd		4,233		4,233
Total	1,228	6,809		6,809

(c) The correct answer is: £ | 620

Working

(1,228 – 608)

(d) The correct answer is: £ | 1,070

Working

(7,879 – 6,809)

(e)

	✓
Debit	
Credit	✓

Task 8.6

(a) **Cash book – credit side**

Details	Cash £	Bank £	VAT £	Trade payables £	Cash purchases £	Motor expenses £
Balance b/f		16,942				
B Smithson Ltd	240		40		200	
H Hamnet	192		32		160	
Renee Reid	320				320	
Tenon Ltd		3,600		3,600		
Vernon Motor Repairs		48	8			40
Total	752	20,590	80	3,600	680	40

BPP LEARNING MEDIA

(b) Cash book – debit side

Details	Cash £	Bank £	VAT £	Trade receivables £
Balance b/f	1,325			
G Brownlow		749		749
S Barnett		300		300
Total	1,325	1,049		1,049

(c) The correct answer is: £ 573

Working

(1,325 – 752 = 573)

(d) The correct answer is: £ 19,541

Working

(20,590 – 1,049 = 19,541)

(e)

	✓
Debit	
Credit	✓

Task 8.7

Cash book – debit side

Details	Cash £	Bank £	VAT £	Trade receivables £	Cash sales £
Balance b/f	55	1,300			
Whippet's	210		35		175
Ragdoll Ltd		958		958	
Totals	265	2,258	35	958	175
Balance b/d	265	1,165			

Cash book – credit side

Details	Cash £	Bank £	VAT £	Trade payables £	Cash purchases £
Hornsea Ltd		355		355	
Lyndon Plc		738		738	
Balance c/d	265	1,165			
Total	265	2,258		1,093	

Task 8.8

(a) Cash book – debit side

Details	Cash £	Bank £	VAT £	Trade receivables £	Cash sales £
Balance b/f	159	844			
Humber & Co	582		97		485
Ridgely Ltd		2,150		2,150	
Watts Partners		978		978	
Total	741	3,972	97	3,128	485

(b) The correct answer is: £ 180   (£741 – £561)

(c) The correct answer is: £ –113   (£3,972 – £4,085)

Chapter 9

Task 9.1

(a) Receivables ledger

Account name	Amount £	Debit ✓	Credit ✓
S Himms	900	✓	
G Pood	1,500	✓	
M Kitchell	456	✓	
B Crown	1,392	✓	

(b) General ledger

Account name	Amount £	Debit ✓	Credit ✓
Sales	3,540		✓
VAT	708		✓
Receivables ledger control	4,248	✓	

Task 9.2

(a) GENERAL Ledger

Receivables ledger control

Details	Amount £	Details	Amount £
Sales	7,085		
VAT	1,417		

Sales

Details	Amount £	Details	Amount £
		Receivables ledger control	7,085

VAT

Details	Amount £	Details	Amount £
		Receivables ledger control	1,417

(b) Receivables ledger

H Simms   RL 45

Details	Amount £	Details	Amount £
Invoice 0001	1,800		

K Mitchell   RL 30

Details	Amount £	Details	Amount £
Invoice 0003	912		

Task 9.3

(a) Receivables ledger

Account name	Amount £	Debit ✓	Credit ✓
Hoppers Ltd	656.40	✓	
Body Perfect	744.00	✓	

(b) General ledger

Account name	Amount £	Debit ✓	Credit ✓
Sales	1,167.00		✓
VAT	233.40		✓
Receivables ledger control	1,400.40	✓	

Task 9.4

(a) GENERAL LEDGER

Receivables ledger control

Details	Amount £	Details	Amount £
Sales	574.00		
VAT	114.80		

Sales

Details	Amount £	Details	Amount £
		Receivables ledger control	574.00

VAT

Details	Amount £	Details	Amount £
		Receivables ledger control	114.80

(b)   RECEIVABLES LEDGER

Langans Beauty

Details	Amount £	Details	Amount £
Invoice 6240	273.60		

Esporta Leisure

Details	Amount £	Details	Amount £
Invoice 6239	415.20		

Task 9.5

(a)   Receivables ledger

Account name	Amount £	Debit ✓	Credit ✓
Rocks Garden Suppliers	701.76	✓	
Eridge Nurseries	429.30	✓	
Abergaven GC	923.40	✓	
Rother Nurseries	756.00	✓	

(b)   General ledger

Account name	Amount £	Debit ✓	Credit ✓
Sales	2,342.05		✓
VAT	468.41		✓
Receivables ledger control	2,810.46	✓	

Task 9.6

(a) **Receivables ledger**

Account name	Amount £	Debit ✓	Credit ✓
Hoppers Ltd	82.44		✓
Esporta Leisure	107.04		✓
Superior Products	14.16		✓

(b) **General ledger**

Account name	Amount £	Debit ✓	Credit ✓
Sales returns	169.70	✓	
VAT	33.94	✓	
Receivables ledger control	203.64		✓

Task 9.7

(a)

Account name	Amount £	Debit ✓	Credit ✓
Hoppers Ltd	36		✓
Esporta Leisure	72		✓

(b)

Account name	Amount £	Debit ✓	Credit ✓
Discounts allowed	90	✓	
VAT	18	✓	
Receivables ledger control	108		✓

Task 9.8

(a)

	True ✓	False ✓
Rother Nurseries has fully settled their account at 31 January 20XX.		✓
Invoice 08695 should have been included in the payment in order to fully settle the account at 31 January.		✓
The remittance advice has been correctly cast.	✓	
The invoice amounts are included correctly on the remittance advice note.		✓

Tutorial note. Rother Nurseries has not fully settled its account as at 31 January because it has made a mistake in the amount included for invoice 08674. It has included this invoice as £114.78 instead of £214.78, therefore it still owes £100. Invoice 08695 is dated 5 February, so did not form part of the account as at 31 January and was correctly excluded from the payment.

(b)

£	1,212.17

Working

£756.00 + £214.78 + £337.89 − £96.50 = £1,212.17

Task 9.9

(a)

	True ✓	False ✓
Abergaven Garden Centre has included on the remittance advice note all relevant transactions up to 9 February.		✓
The remittance advice note has been correctly cast.		✓
The invoice amounts are included correctly on the remittance advice note.	✓	

Tutorial note. Abergaven Garden Centre has not included its credit notes with its payment. Therefore it has paid too much. The remittance advice has not been correctly cast as the final invoice has been excluded from the casting.

(b)

£	2,136.57

Working

923.40 + 623.56 + 316.58 + 415.76 − 32.50 − 110.23 = £2,136.57

Task 9.10

Account name	Amount £	Debit ✓	Credit ✓
VAT	46.64		✓
Cash sales	233.20		✓
Receivables ledger control	2,018.10		✓

Task 9.11

(a) RECEIVABLES LEDGER

Hoppers Ltd

Details	Amount £	Details	Amount £
Invoice 6237	656.40	Credit note 1476	82.44
		Bank	553.96

Body Perfect

Details	Amount £		Amount £
Invoice 6238	744.00	Bank	706.64

Esporta Leisure

Details	Amount £	Details	Amount £
Invoice 6239	415.20	Credit note 1477	107.04
		Bank	367.20

Langans Beauty

Details	Amount £	Details	Amount £
Invoice 6240	273.60	Bank	273.60

Superior Products

Details	Amount £	Details	Amount £
Invoice 6242	265.20	Credit note 1478	14.16
		Bank	116.70

BPP
LEARNING
MEDIA

ANSWERS

(b) GENERAL LEDGER

Cash

Details	Amount £	Details	Amount £
Sales	233.20		
VAT	46.64		

Bank

Details	Amount £	Details	Amount £
Receivables ledger control	2,018.10		

Receivables ledger control

Details	Amount £	Details	Amount £
Sales	3,438.00	Sales returns	169.70
VAT	687.60	VAT	33.94
		Bank	2,018.10

Sales

Details	Amount £	Details	Amount £
		Receivables ledger control	3,438.00
		Cash	233.20

VAT

Details	Amount £	Details	Amount £
Receivables ledger control	33.94	Receivables ledger control	687.60
		Cash	46.64

Task 9.12

(a) Receivables ledger

Account name	Amount £	Debit ✓	Credit ✓
Henderson & Co	7,349		✓

(b) General ledger

Account name	Amount £	Debit ✓	Credit ✓
Receivables ledger control	7,349		✓
Sales	355		✓
VAT	71		✓

Task 9.13

RECEIVABLES LEDGER

Alpha Services   RL 10

Details	Amount £	Details	Amount £
Balance b/d	253.63	Credit note 551	624.00
Invoice 715	5,190.00	Bank	253.63
Invoice 787	10,020.00		

Task 9.14

(a) Receivables ledger

Account name	Amount £	Debit ✓	Credit ✓
Gringles Co	300	✓	
Lester plc	1,308	✓	
Shrier Goods	2,676	✓	
Abunda Bags	1,992	✓	

(b) General ledger

Account name	Amount £	Debit ✓	Credit ✓
Receivables ledger control	6,276	✓	
Sales	5,230		✓
VAT	1,046		✓

Chapter 10

Task 10.1

(a) Purchases daybook

Date 20XX	Details	Invoice number	Total £	VAT £	Net £
30 June	Seashell Ltd	8971	3,853.20	642.20	3,211.00
30 June	Opal & Co	05119	4,800.00	800.00	4,000.00
		Totals	8,653.20	1,422.20	7,211.00

Workings

Seashell Ltd VAT = 3,211 × 20% = 642.20, Gross = 3,211 + 642.20 = 3,853.20

Opal & Co VAT = 4,800/6 = 800, Net = 4,800 - 800 = 4,000

(b) Payables ledger

Account name	Amount £	Debit ✓	Credit ✓
Seashell Ltd	3,853.20		✓
Opal & Co	4,800.00		✓

Task 10.2

(a)

Account name	Amount £	Debit ✓	Credit ✓
Purchases	2,711.00	✓	
Stationery	314.00	✓	
Packaging	432.00	✓	
VAT	691.40	✓	
Payables ledger control	4,148.40		✓

(b)

Account name	Amount £	Debit ✓	Credit ✓
W J Jones	252		✓

Working

£210 × 20 % = £42, gross = £210 + £42 = £252

Task 10.3

(a) **GENERAL LEDGER**

Payables ledger control

Details	Amount £	Details	Amount £
		Purchases	357.00
		Packaging	268.00
		VAT	125.00

VAT

Details	Amount £	Details	Amount £
Payables ledger control	125.00		

Purchases

Details	Amount £	Details	Amount £
Payables ledger control	357.00		

Packaging

Details	Amount £	Details	Amount £
Payables ledger control	268.00		

(b) **PAYABLES LEDGER**

PJ Phillips

Details	Amount £	Details	Amount £
		Invoice 03576	428.40

Packing Supplies

Details	Amount £	Details	Amount £
		Invoice 28423	321.60

Task 10.4

(a) General ledger

Account name	Amount £	Debit ✓	Credit ✓
Wood purchases	996.10	✓	
Polish/varnish purchases	145.60	✓	
Other purchases	57.40	✓	
VAT	239.82	✓	
Payables ledger control	1,438.92		✓

(b) Payables ledger

Account name	Amount £	Debit ✓	Credit ✓
Calverley Bros	174.72		✓
Cavendish Woods	846.12		✓
Culverden & Co	68.88		✓
Ephraim Supplies	349.20		✓

Task 10.5

(a) General ledger

Account name	Amount £	Debit ✓	Credit ✓
Payables ledger control	667.20	✓	
Purchases returns	444.00		✓
Stationery	112.00		✓
VAT	111.20		✓

(b) Payables ledger

Account name	Amount £	Debit ✓	Credit ✓
K Mates	235.20	✓	
R Jones	134.40	✓	
X & Y Ltd	297.60	✓	

Task 10.6

(a)   GENERAL LEDGER

Payables ledger control

Details	Amount £	Details	Amount £
Purchases returns	222.00	Purchases	2,711.00
Stationery	56.00	Stationery	314.00
VAT	55.60	Packaging	432.00
		VAT	691.40

VAT

Details	Amount £	Details	Amount £
Payables ledger control	691.40	Payables ledger control	55.60

Purchases returns

Details	Amount £	Details	Amount £
		Payables ledger control	222.00

Stationery

Details	Amount £	Details	Amount £
Payables ledger control	314.00	Payables ledger control	56.00

(b)   PAYABLES LEDGER

Phillips

Details	Amount £	Details	Amount £
Credit note 04216	117.60	Invoice 0357	428.40
		Invoice 0358	495.60

Wallace

Details	£	Details	£
Credit note CN0643	67.20	Invoice 1342	252.00
		Invoice 1350	124.80

Olivia Ltd

Details	£	Details	£
Credit note CN1102	148.80	Invoice 55773	748.80

Task 10.7

(a)

Account name	Amount £	Debit ✓	Credit ✓
Purchases	90.00	✓	
VAT	18.00	✓	
Payables ledger control	1,357.07	✓	

(b)

Account name	Amount £	Debit ✓	Credit ✓
Time Ltd	1,105.07	✓	
WFF Ltd	252.00	✓	

Task 10.8

(a) **Payables ledger**

Account name	Amount £	Debit ✓	Credit ✓
Frankie's Leatherware	12,348		✓
Casaubon's	3,924		✓

(b) **General ledger**

Account name	Amount £	Debit ✓	Credit ✓
Purchases	13,560	✓	
VAT	2,712	✓	
Payables ledger control	16,272		✓

Task 10.9

(a) **Payables ledger**

Account name	Amount £	Debit ✓	Credit ✓
Trenter Ltd	36	✓	
WJ Jones	72	✓	

(b) **General ledger**

Account name	Amount £	Debit ✓	Credit ✓
Payables ledger control	108	✓	
Discounts received	90		✓
VAT	18		✓

Task 10.10

(a) **Payables ledger**

Account name	Amount £	Debit ✓	Credit ✓
Casaubon's	2,445	✓	

(b) **General ledger**

Account name	Amount £	Debit ✓	Credit ✓
Payables ledger control	2,445	✓	
Purchases	510	✓	
VAT	102	✓	

Task 10.11

What will be the entries in the general ledger?

Account name	Amount £	Debit ✓	Credit ✓
Payables ledger control	2,492	✓	
Receivables ledger control	4,368		✓
Cash sales	295		✓
VAT	59		✓

Chapter 11

Task 11.1

£	68.34

Tutorial note. The cash required to replenish the petty cash box is equal to the total of the vouchers in the petty cash box.

Task 11.2

(a) **Petty cash book**

Date 20XX	Details	Amount £	Date 20XX	Details	Amount £	VAT £	Travel £	Office expenses £
24 Jan	Balance b/f	120.00	27 Jan	Paper	7.12	1.18		5.94
			29 Jan	Coffee	3.99			3.99
			29 Jan	Taxi	10.72	1.78	8.94	
			29 Jan	Balance c/d	98.17			
	Total	120.00		Totals	120.00	2.96	8.94	9.93

(b)

£	21.83

Working £120 – £98.17 = £21.83

Task 11.3

(a)

£	16

Working

	£
Opening balance	22
Cash from bank	53
Less: expenditure during month	(16)
balance at end of month	59

Therefore 75 – 59 = £16 required to restore the imprest level

(b)

	✓
Debit	✓
Credit	

Task 11.4

Petty cash control

Date	Details	Amount £	Date	Details	Amount £
1 Jan	Balance b/f	150.00	31 Jan	Expenditure	101.50
			31 Jan	Balance c/d	48.50
	Total	150.00		Total	150.00
1 Feb	Balance b/d	48.50			

Task 11.5

(a) – (c)

Petty cash book

Date	Details	Amount £	Date	Details	Total £	Stationery £	Postage £	Motor fuel £
1 Nov	Bal b/f	100	7 Nov	Postage stamps	20		20	
			15 Nov	Pens and pencils	18	18		
			22 Nov	Petrol	10			10
			30 Nov	Envelopes	15	15		
			30 Nov	Balance c/d	37			
	Total	100		Total	100	33	20	10
1 Dec	Balance c/d	37						

Task 11.6

(a) – (b)

Petty cash book

Debit side		Credit side					
Details	**Amount £**	**Details**	**Amount £**	**VAT £**	**Postage £**	**Travel £**	**Cleaning £**
Bal b/f	175.00	Post Office	30.00		30.00		
		Window cleaning	30.72	5.12			25.60
		MegaBus	29.50			29.50	
		Balance c/d	84.78				
Total	175.00	Total	175.00	5.12	30.00	29.50	25.60

Task 11.7

Petty cash reimbursement		
Date: 30.09.20XX		
Amount required to restore the cash in the petty cash box	£	240.24

Tutorial note. The amount of cash required to restore the petty cash is the imprest amount less the cash remaining in the box: £250 – £9.76 = £240.24.

Task 11.8

(a) – (b)

Petty cash book

Debit side		Credit side					
Details	**Amount £**	**Details**	**Amount £**	**VAT £**	**Postage £**	**Travel £**	**Stationery £**
Balance b/f	150.00	Tom's Taxi	18.00			18.00	
		Post Office	30.00		30.00		
		SMP Stationery	43.20	7.20			36.00
		Balance c/d	58.80				
Total	150.00	Total	150.00	7.20	30.00	18.00	36.00

Task 11.9

Petty cash reimbursement		
Date: 31.07.20XX		
Amount required to restore the cash in the petty cash box	£	196.55

Task 11.10

(a)   General ledger

Account name	Amount £	Debit ✓	Credit ✓
Petty cash	108.32		✓
VAT	15.52	✓	
Office expenses	15.20	✓	
Stationery	32.60	✓	
Maintenance	45.00	✓	

(b)   The answer is: | Petty cash |

Tutorial note. The credit entry to petty cash would not be needed if the petty cash book was itself part of the general ledger double entry system.

Task 11.11

	✓
Imprest system	
Non-imprest system	✓

Task 11.12

(a) – (b)

Petty cash book

Debit side		Credit side					
Details	Amount £	Details	Amount £	VAT £	Postage £	Travel £	Stationery £
Balance b/f	75.23	Taxi	9.00			9.00	
Bank	60.00	Post Office	15.00		15.00		
		Suzie's Stationery	43.20	7.20			36.00
Balance b/d		Balance c/d	68.03				
Total	135.23	Total	135.23	7.20	15.00	9.00	36.00

(c) The correct answer is: | **£** | 68.03 |

Tutorial note. The balance c/d on the petty cash book above is the amount of cash remaining in the petty cash tin on Friday. This is a **non-imprest** system of managing petty cash because Lucy tops up the balance by £60 each week independently of the petty cash expenditure.

Task 11.13

(a) – (b)

Petty cash-book

Details	Amount £	Details	Amount £	VAT £	Postage £	Stationery £
Balance b/f	175.00	Printer cartridges	17.40	2.90		14.50
		Stamps	12.60		12.60	
		Staplers	18.90	3.15		15.75
		Balance c/d	126.10			
Total	175.00	Totals	175.00	6.05	12.60	30.25

Working £18.90 × 20/120 = £3.15 VAT

(c)

General ledger accounts	✓
Stamps	
Stationery	✓
Petty cash-book	
Petty cash control	
Postage	✓
Staplers	
VAT	✓

(d)

	✓
Remittance advice note	
Cheque requisition form	✓
Petty cash claim	
Customer statement	

(e) | **£** | 48.90 |

Working £17.40 + £12.60 + £18.90 = £48.90

BPP PRACTICE ASSESSMENT 1

INTRODUCTION TO BOOKKEEPING

Time allowed: 1.5 hours

Introduction to Bookkeeping (ITBK)
BPP practice assessment 1

Introduction

The tasks in this assessment are set in different business situations where the following apply:

- Businesses use a variety of bookkeeping systems.
- Double entry takes place in the general ledger.
- The VAT rate is 20%.

Task 1 (10 marks)

This task is about manual and digital bookkeeping systems.

(a) **Identify which document or report would be used for each of the purposes below.**

(4 marks)

To summarise assets and liabilities and report the business's financial position at the end of the accounting period.	Gap 1
To identify whether or not there is an imbalance in debit and credit entries in the nominal ledger.	Gap 2
To summarise income and expenses for a period.	Gap 3
To identify which credit suppliers are due for payment.	Gap 4

Gap 1 options	✓
Trial balance	
Statement of profit or loss	
Trade payables listing	
Statement of financial position	✓

Gap 2 options	✓
Trial balance	✓
Statement of profit or loss	
Trade payables listing	
Statement of financial position	

Gap 3 options	✓
Trial balance	
Statement of profit or loss	✓
Trade payables listing	
Statement of financial position	

Gap 4 options	✓
Trial balance	
Statement of profit or loss	
Trade payables listing	✓
Statement of financial position	

Product codes for a range of furniture follow the format below:

- First two letters of the product colour.
- First two letters of the product type.
- A sequential number for each product.

The last product code created is shown in the table below.

(b)   **Create a product code for each of the two new products.**   (2 marks)

Date 20XX	Product	Product code
14 May	Green desk	GRDE304
16 May	Beige chairs	BECH101
18 May	Brown tables	BRTA102

(c)   **Identify whether each of the following statements regarding manual bookkeeping systems are TRUE or FALSE.**   (2 marks)

Statement	True ✓	False ✓
A cash book is always a book of prime entry but never part of the double-entry bookkeeping system.		✓
A petty cash book is not part of the double-entry bookkeeping system if there is a Bank account in the general ledger.		✓

(d)   **Complete the following statement about digital bookkeeping systems by selecting the appropriate option in each gap below.**   (2 marks)

Digital systems will ...	Gap 1
...but will not...	Gap 2

Gap 1 options	✓
automatically balance the cash book	
automatically alert the bookkeeper to all errors	✓

Gap 2 options	✓
process recurring entries.	✓
ensure that all underlying cash book entries are correct.	

Task 2 (10 marks)

This task is about principles of double-entry bookkeeping.

The following accounts are in the bookkeeping system.

(a)   **Identify the classification of each account.**   (4 marks)

Property	Gap 1
Electricity expense	Gap 2
Trade payables	Gap 3
Sales revenue	Gap 4

Gap 1 options	✓
Asset	—
Liability	
Income	
Expense	

Gap 2 options	✓
Asset	
Liability	
Income	
Expense	✓

Gap 3 options	✓
Asset	
Liability	✓
Income	
Expense	

Gap 4 options	✓
Asset	
Liability	
Income	✓
Expense	

The asset accounts total £180,340 and the liabilities account totals £130,560.

(b) **Calculate the amount of capital in the business. Do NOT use a minus sign or brackets.**

(1 mark)

£ | 49,780

The transactions below have been entered into the bookkeeping system.

(c) **Identify the dual effect of each transaction by dragging the appropriate description into the table below. You should ignore VAT in this task.** (5 marks)

Transaction	Dual effect
Purchased office furniture on credit	3
Incurred expenses and settled them in cash	2
Sold goods on credit	4
Owner took drawings in cash	5
Received money from a credit customer which reduced a bank overdraft	1

Description
Increase in both an asset and income
Increase in expenses and decrease in an asset
Increase in both an asset and a liability
Decrease in both an asset and a liability
Increase in drawings and decrease in cash

Task 3 (10 marks)

This task is about processing customer invoices or credit notes and entering in daybooks.

A sales invoice is being prepared from the delivery note below. The customer benefits from a 5% bulk discount.

> **Sandy Ltd**
> **Delivery note DN8965**
>
> To: Cuthbert Ltd   Customer ref CUTH01
>   1 April 20XX
>
> 3400 units............. Product K314
> Price before discount: £2.20 per unit, plus VAT.

(a)   Calculate the amounts to be included in the invoice.   (5 marks)

	£
Amount before discount	7,480
Bulk discount	374
Amount after discount	7,106
VAT @ 20%	1421.2
Total	8,527.2

(b)   Identify the daybook in which the invoice will be entered.   (1 mark)

Daybook	✓
Sales daybook	✓
Sales returns daybook	
Purchases daybook	
Purchases returns daybook	
Discounts allowed daybook	
Discounts received daybook	

(c)   Complete the entry in the daybook.   (4 marks)

Date 20XX	Customer code	Customer	Invoice number	Total £	VAT £	Net £	K313 £	K314 £	K315 £
1 April	CUTH01	Cuthbert Ltd	2026	8,527	1421	7,106		7,106	

Task 4 (10 marks)

This task is about processing receipts from customers.

LMN Ltd has received a cheque for £1,662 from Horton Ltd in full settlement of the two invoices and credit note below.

LMN Ltd	
To: Horton Ltd	
7 November 20XX	
Invoice No: 8499	
	£
80 units Product G82	960.00
VAT @ 20%	192.00
Total	1,152.00
Terms: Net monthly	

LMN Ltd	
To: Horton Ltd	
9 November 20XX	
Invoice No: 8500	
	£
110 units Product Z49	825.00
VAT @ 20%	165.00
Total	990.00
Terms: Net monthly	

LMN Ltd	
To: Horton Ltd	
16 November 20XX	
Credit note No: 92	
	£
20 units Product Z49	150.00
VAT @ 20%	30.00
Total	180.00
Terms: Net monthly	

(a) **Complete the following statement about the accuracy of the amount received by selecting the appropriate option in each gap below.** (2 marks)

Horton Ltd has.......	
so	

Gap 1 options	✓
underpaid the amount owing	
overpaid the amount owing	
paid the correct amount	

Gap 2 options	✓
a request for a further payment should be made.	
there is no balance outstanding.	
a refund should be offered.	

Desborough plc has offered a customer a 4% discount for payment of all the outstanding invoices detailed below, by the end of the month.

(b) Calculate the amount that should be paid by the end of the month to settle:

- each invoice
- the total of all the invoices. (4 marks)

Outstanding invoices	Total £	VAT £	Net £	Amount to be paid by the end of the month
2071	1,740.00	290.00	1,450.00	
2095	450.00	75.00	375.00	
2110	624.00	104.00	520.00	
			Total	

Rupal Ltd has received a cheque for £1,909.95 and the remittance advice below from a customer. The customer's terms of payment are net monthly.

Remittance advice	
Invoice	£
2021	220.50
2029	375.88
2036	790.74
2040	522.83
Total	1,909.95

Company policy is to allocate any underpayment as a part payment and to query any overpayment.

(c) Allocate the amount received in the customer report below, by selecting the appropriate action to take for each transaction. (4 marks)

Transaction type	Details	Amount £	Action
Balance b/f		596.38	Gap 1
Invoice 2036	Delivery note 4893	795.60	Gap 2
Invoice 2040	Delivery note 4902	647.83	Gap 3
Credit note 152	Re overcharge in invoice 2040	125.00	Gap 4

Gap 1 options	✓
Allocate full amount	
Allocate part payment	
Query overpayment	

Gap 2 options	✓
Allocate full amount	
Allocate part payment	
Query overpayment	

Gap 3 options	✓
Allocate full amount	
Allocate part payment	
Query overpayment	

Gap 4 options	✓
Allocate full amount	
Allocate part payment	
Query overpayment	

Task 5 (10 marks)

This task is about processing supplier invoices or credit notes and entering in daybooks.

The supplier invoice below has been checked, authorised and coded.

<table>
<tr><td colspan="2" align="center">Cameron Ltd</td></tr>
<tr><td>To: Larka plc
Invoice No: 4359</td><td>Date: 21 August 20XX</td></tr>
<tr><td></td><td align="right">£</td></tr>
<tr><td>200 units of Product GK42 @ £4.70 per metre</td><td align="right">940.00</td></tr>
<tr><td>VAT @ 20%</td><td align="right">188.00</td></tr>
<tr><td>Total</td><td align="right">1,128.00</td></tr>
<tr><td colspan="2">Terms: Net monthly</td></tr>
<tr><td>Checked by: CR</td><td>Authorised by: DC</td></tr>
<tr><td>General ledger code: 7492</td><td>Supplier code: CAM63</td></tr>
</table>

(a)   Enter the invoice in the digital bookkeeping system by:
   • selecting the correct module option
   • making the necessary entries (6 marks)

Daybook	✓
Sales daybook	✓
Sales returns daybook	
Purchases daybook	
Purchases returns daybook	
Discounts allowed daybook	
Discounts received daybook	

Date 20XX	Supplier code	Supplier	General ledger code	Invoice number	Net £	VAT Code
21 August	CAM 63	Cameron Ltd	7492	4359	940	Option 1

Option 1	✓
VAT1 – Exempt	
VAT2 – 0%	
VAT3 – 5%	
VAT4 – 20%	✓

The purchase order and invoice below relate to goods supplied by Bow Products.

Larka plc
Purchase order No. P2930

To: Bow Products   23 August 20XX

Please supply:

95 boxes of unit VL

Agreed price: £5.24 per box

Agreed terms: net 30 days

Bow Products
Invoice 9429

To: Larka plc   19 August 20XX
Purchase order reference: P2903

	£
95 boxes of unit AQ @ £5.24 per box	497.80
VAT @ 20%	124.45
Total	622.25

Terms of payment: net 30 days

(b)   **Identify FOUR discrepancies in the invoice.**   (4 marks)

Discrepancy	✓
Details of the quantity supplied	
Unit code of the product	✓
Purchase order reference	
Date of invoice	✓
Unit price	
Net amount	✓
VAT amount	✓
Terms of payment	

Task 6 (10 marks)

This task is about processing payments to suppliers.

An invoice dated 12 June has been received from a supplier for £10,200 including VAT. The supplier's terms of payment are:

- 30 days net or
- 3% discount for payment received within 20 days of date of invoice or
- 4% discount for payment received within 10 days of date of invoice.

(a) (i) **Identify the date by which the supplier should receive payment if no discount is taken.**

	✓
22 June	
30 June	
2 July	
12 July	✓
15 July	
31 July	

(ii) **Identify the amount to be paid, and the date by which the supplier should receive payment, for each of the terms of payment offered below.**   (5 marks)

Terms of payment	Amount to be paid £	Date by which supplier should receive payment	
Payment within 20 days	9 8 9 4	2 July	▼
Payment within 10 days	9 7 9 2	22 June	▼

Date options
22 June
30 June
2 July
12 July
15 July
31 July

A statement of account received from another supplier, Trewlin Products, does not reconcile with the supplier report below. The statement of account shows an amount outstanding of £10,513. This amount does not include the two cheques dated 30 and 31 July which were received by the supplier after the statement had been prepared.

(b) Identify which FOUR amounts were included in the two cheques by entering a tick next to the appropriate amounts. **(4 marks)**

	Supplier report Trewlin Products				✓
Date 20XX	Transaction type	Details	£		
1 July	BAL	Balance b/d	2,240		
4 July	SC	Credit note 416	456		
13 July	SI	Invoice 5302	1,930		
17 July	SI	Invoice 5335	1,253		
18 July	SI	Invoice 5350	562		
19 July	SI	Invoice 5366	2,987	✓	
20 July	SI	Invoice 5382	606	✓	
22 July	SI	Invoice 5415	249	✓	
22 July	SI	Invoice 5419	1,142	✓	
30 July	BT	Cheque 0205029	1,784		
31 July	BT	Cheque 0205041	1,859		

(c) Calculate the amount that should be paid to settle the remaining balance of the account. **(1 mark)**

£ [   ]

Task 7 (8 marks)

This task is about processing transactions in the cash book.

Two amounts have been paid today as shown in the receipts below.

BHY Ltd Receipt THI394	
Date: 31 October 20XX	
Building insurance (annual) Exempt from VAT. Cheque received for full amount	£3,060.80

WTR Ltd Receipt 1029
Date: 31 October 20XX
Six office desks (product code OA23) £1,260 including VAT @ 20% Paid in full by debit card.

(a)   Enter the transactions in the digital bookkeeping system by:

- selecting the correct module option
- making the necessary entries.   (7 marks)

Module option	✓
Cash book – receipts	
Cash book – payments	
Petty cash book – receipts	
Petty cash book - payments	

Date 20XX	Details	General ledger code	Document number	Net £	VAT code
31 October	BHY Ltd	Option 1	THI394		Option 2
31 October	WTR Ltd	Option 1	1029		Option 2

Option 1
1330 – Office furniture
2110 – Trade payables
6100 – Purchases
6220 – Insurance expenses

Option 2
VAT1 – Exempt
VAT2 – 0%
VAT3 – 5%
VAT4 – 20%

At the end of the month the debit side of the cash book totalled £16,420.91 and the credit side totalled £18,542.72.

(b)   **Calculate the bank balance. Use a minus sign if your calculations indicate an overdrawn bank balance, e.g. -123.**   (1 mark)

£	

Task 8 (6 marks)

This task is about processing transactions in the petty cash book.

An organisation keeps an analytical petty cash book and withdraws £250 from the bank on the first day of each month to top up the petty cash float.

On 1 December there was £73.26 in the petty cash box. Later that day the usual amount was withdrawn from the bank to top up the petty cash float. During the month petty cash purchases totalled £242.56.

(a)   **Identify the entry required in the petty cash book to record the closing balance on 31 December.**   (3 marks)

Details	Amount £	Debit ✓	Credit ✓
Option 1	7·44		✓

Option 1
Balance carried down
Balance brought down

The first petty cash purchase in December is shown below.

Petty cash voucher No 892
1 December 20XX
Coffee, tea and milk purchased from General Stores £18.60 plus VAT.
Receipt attached.

(b) **Complete the entry in the petty cash book.** (3 marks)

Date 20XX	Details	Total £	VAT £	Net £
1 December	General Stores	22.32	3.72	18.60

Task 9 (6 marks)

This task is about processing recurring entries.

A new bank payment has been authorised as shown in the note below.

I have today authorised a monthly standing order relating to business rates paid to LCR Council.

Please set up a recurring entry to pay the total amount of £1,980 in equal instalments of £165, starting on 15 February.

The transaction is exempt from VAT.

Len Preedy

1 February 20XX

(a) **Set up the recurring entry.** (5 marks)

Transaction type	Details	Start date 20XX	Frequency	Recurrences	Amount £	VAT code
Bank payment	Option 1	15 February	Option 2	12	165	Option 3

Option 1	
250 – Bank	✓
270 – Cash	
810 – Business rates	
840 - Rent	

Option 2	
Weekly	
Bi-weekly	
Monthly	✓
Quarterly	

Option 3
VAT1 – Exempt ✓
VAT2 – 0%
VAT3 – 5%
VAT 4 – 20%

The following day the digital bookkeeping system displays the message below.

Do you want to process recurring entries today?

(b) **Process ONE recurring entry by clicking on the appropriate amount.** (1 mark)

Payment type	Details	Next posting	Posting made	Amount £
STO	YPT Ltd	2 Feb 20XX	4	760
DD	LCR Council	15 Feb 20XX	0	165
DD	TNA Ltd	18 Feb 20XX	10	545
STO	BMW Ltd	25 Feb 20XX	3	238

Task 10 (10 marks)

This task is about transferring data from the books of prime entry.

These are the totals of the purchases returns daybook at Carlton Electra.

Details	Total £	VAT £	Net £
Totals	4,947.36	824.56	4,122.80

(a) **Show the entries to be made in the general ledger accounts below.** (6 marks)

Account name	Amount £	Debit ✓	Credit ✓
Payables ledger control	4947.36		✓
VAT	824.56	✓	
Purchases returns	4,122.80	✓	

The discounts allowed daybook has been totalled and all amounts have been transferred to the relevant general ledger accounts. One of the transactions relates to a credit note for £110 plus VAT sent to Peters Ltd.

(b) Identify the ledger in which the credit note will be entered. (1 mark)

Ledger	✓
General	
Payables	✓
Receivables	

(c) Enter the credit note in the relevant ledger account. (3 marks)

Account name	Amount £	Debit ✓	Credit ✓
Peter's ltd	132		✓

Account name
Carlton Electra
Discounts allowed
Discounts received
Purchases
Purchases returns
Payables ledger control
Peters Ltd
Receivables ledger control

Task 11 (10 marks)

This task is about totalling and balancing ledger accounts.

The receivables account below is ready to be totalled and balanced at the end of November.

B Martin

Date 20XX	Details	Amount £	Date 20XX	Details	Amount £
1 Nov	Balance b/d	11,282	15 Nov	Bank payment	10,162
21 Nov	Invoice	22,304	28 Nov	Credit note	1,120
29 Nov	Invoice	14,750		Bal c/d	37,294
	Total	48,336		Total	48,336

(a) Identify the entry required to record the closing balance on 30 November: (3 marks)

Details	Amount £	Debit ✓	Credit ✓
Bal c/d	39,294		✓

Option 1	✓
Balance brought down	
Balance carried down	✓

(b) Calculate the total amount that will be entered in each debit and credit column after the closing balance has been recorded. (1 mark)

£ 48,336

The following two accounts are in the general ledger at close of day on 30 November.

Account GL040

Date 20XX	Details	Amount £	Date 20XX	Details	Amount £
5 Nov	Bank	2,040	10 Nov	Cash	76
14 Nov	Cash	988			

Account GL150

Date 20XX	Details	Amount £	Date 20XX	Details	Amount £
16 Nov	Cash	69	4 Nov	Bank	680
			11 Nov	Cash	375

(c) Identify the entries required to record the opening balance in each account on 1 December. (6 marks)

Account code	Details	Amount £	Debit ✓	Credit ✓
GL040	Option 1	2952		✓
GL150	Option 1	986	✓	

Option 1	✓
Balance brought down	✓
Balance carried down	

BPP PRACTICE ASSESSMENT 1

INTRODUCTION TO BOOKKEEPING

ANSWERS

Introduction to Bookkeeping (ITBK)
BPP practice assessment 1

Task 1

(a)

To summarise assets and liabilities and report the business's financial position at the end of the accounting period.	Statement of financial position
To identify whether or not there is an imbalance in debit and credit entries in the nominal ledger.	Trial balance
To summarise income and expenses for a period.	Statement of profit or loss
To identify which credit suppliers are due for payment.	Trade payables listing

(b)

Date 20XX	Product	Product code
14 May	Green desk	GRDE304
16 May	Beige chairs	BECH305
18 May	Brown tables	BRTA306

(c)

Statement	True ✓	False ✓
A cash book is always a book of prime entry but never part of the double-entry bookkeeping system.		✔
A petty cash book is not part of the double-entry bookkeeping system if there is a Bank account in the general ledger.	✔	

The cash book and petty cash book are books of prime entry. They can also be part of the double-entry bookkeeping system.

If there is a separate Bank accounting in the general ledger, then the petty cash book and cash book do not form part of the double-entry bookkeeping system.

(d)

Digital systems will ...	automatically balance the cash book
...but will not...	ensure that all underlying cash book entries are correct.

Digital systems will not alert bookkeepers to all errors. For example, if a transaction is omitted from the nominal ledger, the system will not be able to identify this.

A digital accounting system is able to process recurring entries.

ANSWERS

Task 2

(a)

Property	Asset
Electricity expense	Expense
Trade payables	Liability
Sales revenue	Income

(b)

£	49,780

Working: £180,340 minus £130,560 = £49,780.

(c)

Transaction	Dual effect
Purchased office furniture on credit	Increase in both an asset and a liability
Incurred expenses and settled them in cash	Increase in expenses and decrease in an asset
Sold goods on credit	Increase in both an asset and income
Owner took drawings in cash	Increase in drawings and decrease in cash
Received money from a credit customer which reduced a bank overdraft	Decrease in both an asset and a liability

Task 3

(a)

	£
Amount before discount	7,480.00
Bulk discount	(374.00)
Amount after discount	7,106.00
VAT @ 20%	1,421.20
Total	8,527.20

(b)

Daybook	✓
Sales daybook	✓
Sales returns daybook	
Purchases daybook	
Purchases returns daybook	
Discounts allowed daybook	
Discounts received daybook	

(c)

Date 20XX	Customer code	Customer	Invoice number	Total £	VAT £	Net £	K313 £	K314 £	K315 £
1 April	CUTH01	Cuthbert Ltd	2026	8,527.20	1,421.20	7,106.00		7,106.00	

Task 4

(a)

Horton Ltd has.......	underpaid the amount owing
so	a request for a further payment should be made.

Horton Ltd should have paid £1,962 to settle the two invoices less the credit note. Only £1,662 has been paid, therefore a further £300 remains outstanding.

(b)

Outstanding invoices	Total £	VAT £	Net £	Amount to be paid by the end of the month
2071	1,740.00	290.00	1,450.00	1,670.40
2095	450.00	75.00	375.00	432.00
2110	624.00	104.00	520.00	599.04
			Total	2,701.44

(c)

Transaction type	Details	Amount £	Action
Balance b/f		596.38	Allocate full amount
Invoice 2036	Delivery note 4893	795.60	Allocate part payment
Invoice 2040	Delivery note 4902	647.83	Allocate full amount
Credit note 152	Re overcharge in invoice 2040	125.00	Allocate full amount

Workings:

Balance b/d = £220.50 + £375.88 = £596.38, therefore full amount allocated

Invoice 2036 only £790.74 was paid instead of £795.60, therefore allocate part payment

Invoice 2040 for £647.83 less credit note 152 for £125.00 is £522.83 therefore, allocate full amount to both

Task 5

(a)

Daybook	✓
Sales daybook	
Sales returns daybook	
Purchases daybook	✓
Purchases returns daybook	
Discounts allowed daybook	
Discounts received daybook	

Date 20XX	Supplier code	Supplier	General ledger code	Invoice number	Net £	VAT Code
21 August	CAM63	Cameron Ltd	7492	4359	940.00	VAT4 – 20%

(b)

Discrepancy	✓
Details of the quantity supplied	
Unit code of the product	✓
Purchase order reference	✓
Date of invoice	✓
Unit price	
Net amount	
VAT amount	✓
Terms of payment	

The product unit should have the reference 'VL' instead of 'AQ'. The purchase order is dated 23 August, therefore the invoice should be prepared after this date.

The net amount should be calculated as 95 boxes @ £5.24 per box = £497.80. The VAT should then be £497.80 @ 20% = £99.56. Therefore, the net amount is correctly stated, however, the VAT is incorrectly stated.

Task 6

(a) (i)

	✓
22 June	
30 June	
2 July	
12 July	✓
15 July	
31 July	

(ii)

Terms of payment	Amount to be paid £	Date by which supplier should receive payment
Payment within 20 days	**9,894**	**2 July**
Payment within 10 days	9,792	22 June

The invoice amount was £10,200 including VAT, therefore the net amount is £8,500 (£10,200 × 100/120).

If a 3% discount is taken then the amount payable is £9,894 (£8,500 × 97% × 1.2).

If a 4% discount is taken then the amount payable is £9,792 (£8,500 × 96% × 1.2).

(b)

Supplier report Trewlin Products				✓
Date 20XX	Transaction type	Details	£	
1 July	BAL	Balance b/d	2,240	✓
4 July	SC	Credit note 416	456	✓
13 July	SI	Invoice 5302	1,930	
17 July	SI	Invoice 5335	1,253	✓
18 July	SI	Invoice 5350	562	
19 July	SI	Invoice 5366	2,987	
20 July	SI	Invoice 5382	606	✓
22 July	SI	Invoice 5415	249	
22 July	SI	Invoice 5419	1,142	
30 July	BT	Cheque 0205029	1,784	
31 July	BT	Cheque 0205041	1,859	

Workings:

£2,240 less £456 = £1,784

£1,253 + £606 = £1,859

(c)

£	6,870

Tutorial note:

Calculated by adding up the remaining unpaid balances per the supplier's report.

Task 7

(a)

Module option	✓
Cash book – receipts	
Cash book – payments	✓
Petty cash book – receipts	
Petty cash book - payments	

Date 20XX	Details	General ledger code	Document number	Net £	VAT code
31 October	BHY Ltd	6220 - Insurance expenses	THI394	3,060.80	VAT1 – Exempt
31 October	WTR Ltd	1330 – Office furniture	1029	1,050.00	VAT4 – 20%

Working:

WTR Ltd £1,260 x 100/120 = £1,050.00

(b)

£	-2,121.81

Task 8

(a)

Details	Amount £	Debit ✓	Credit ✓
Balance c/d	80.70		✓

Note that the phrase 'Balance c/d' is the description used to record the closing balance on the last day of the month.

Working: £250 + £73.26 - £242.56 = £80.70

(b)

Date 20XX	Details	Total £	VAT £	Net £
1 December	General Stores	22.32	3.72	18.60

Task 9

(a)

Transaction type	Details	Start date 20XX	Frequency	Recurrences	Amount £	VAT code
Bank payment	810 – Business rates	15 February	Monthly	12	165	VAT1 – Exempt

(b)

Payment type	Details	Next posting	Posting made	Amount £
STO	YPT Ltd	2 Feb 20XX	4	**760**
DD	LCR Council	15 Feb 20XX	0	165
DD	TNA Ltd	18 Feb 20XX	10	545
STO	BMW Ltd	25 Feb 20XX	3	238

Task 10

(a)

Account name	Amount £	Debit ✓	Credit ✓
Payables ledger control	4,947.36	✓	
VAT	824.56		✓
Purchases returns	4,122.80		✓

(b)

Ledger	✓
General	
Payables	
Receivables	✓

(c)

Account name	Amount £	Debit ✓	Credit ✓
Peters Ltd	132.00		✓

Working

£110 + (£110 × 20% = £22) = £132

Task 11

(a)

Details	Amount £	Debit ✓	Credit ✓
Balance c/d	37,054		✓

(b)

£	48,336

Working **(a)** and **(b)**

Date 20XX	Details	Amount £	Date 20XX	Details	Amount £
1 Nov	Balance b/d	11,282	15 Nov	Bank payment	10,162
21 Nov	Invoice	22,304	28 Nov	Credit note	1,120
29 Nov	Invoice	14,750	30 Nov	Balance c/d	37,054
	Total	48,336		Total	48,336

(c)

Account code	Details	Amount £	Debit ✓	Credit ✓
GL040	Balance b/d	2,952	✓	
GL150	Balance b/d	986		✓

Workings

Account GL040

Date 20XX	Details	Amount £	Date 20XX	Details	Amount £
5 Nov	Bank	2,040	10 Nov	Cash	76
14 Nov	Cash	988	30 Nov	Balance c/d	2,952
	Total	3,028		Total	3,028
1 Dec	Balance b/d	2,952			

Account GL150

Date 20XX	Details	Amount £	Date 20XX	Details	Amount £
16 Nov	Cash	69	4 Nov	Bank	680
30 Nov	Balance c/d	986	11 Nov	Cash	375
	Total	1,055		Total	1,055
			1 Dec	Balance b/d	986

BPP PRACTICE ASSESSMENT 2

INTRODUCTION TO BOOKKEEPING

Time allowed: 1.5 hours

BPP
LEARNING
MEDIA

201

Introduction to Bookkeeping (ITBK)
BPP Practice Assessment 2

Introduction

The tasks in this assessment are set in different business situations where the following apply:

- Businesses use a variety of bookkeeping systems.
- Double entry takes place in the general ledger.
- The VAT rate is 20%.

Task 1 (10 marks)

This task is about manual and digital bookkeeping systems.

(a) **Identify which document or report would be used for each of the purposes below.**

(4 marks)

Details the items requested by the customer; includes a product description, product code, quantity required and the agreed terms (price, discount if relevant).	Gap 1
Detailing money paid in and paid out of the bank account for a given period, and stating the opening and closing balance at the start and end of the period.	Gap 2
Lists items sent to a business; includes customer and supplier details, date of despatch, the product code, the quantity, and the corresponding order number.	Gap 3
Details the items provided to credit customers; includes a description of the items supplied, product code, amount due including VAT/discounts where appropriate.	Gap 4

Gap 1 options	✓
Bank statement	
Customer order	✓
Delivery note	
Invoice	

Gap 2 options	✓
Bank statement	✓
Customer order	
Delivery note	
Invoice	

Gap 3 options	✓
Bank statement	
Customer order	
Delivery note	✓
Invoice	

Gap 4 options	✓
Bank statement	
Customer order	
Delivery note	
Invoice	✓

The digital bookkeeping system that you use creates customer codes using the following format:

- First five letters of the customer name, followed by two numerical digits.

The current customer accounts in the receivables ledger are:

Customer name	Customer account code
Benjamin & Co	BENJA01
Grantham Ltd	GRANT01
Granthorp and George	GRANT02
Priya Ltd	PRIYA01
Sanderson Services	SANDE01
Weathersport Ltd	WEATH01

The two new customer accounts show below require a customer account code.

(b) **Enter the relevant account codes for each customer that the digital bookkeeping system will create.** (2 marks)

Customer name	Customer account code
Hawkins Ltd	HAWKI01
Sanderstone & Co	SANDE02

(c) **Identify the book of prime entry being described in the statement below.** (1 mark)

A daybook detailing prompt payment discounts given to credit customers.

	✓
Discount allowed daybook	✓
Discount received daybook	
Purchase daybook	
Sales daybook	

(d) **Identify whether the following statements regarding bookkeeping systems are true or false.** (3 marks)

Statement	True ✓	False ✓
Some transactions can be entered in the general ledger as a single entry without giving rise to an error in the accounting records.		✓
In most digital accounting systems, transactions relating to receivables and payables are entered once in the sales daybook or purchases daybook. The relevant control account and ledger account are then automatically updated to reflect the postings.	✓	
In a manual accounting system, there is more scope for error as automatic entries and recurring entries are not possible.	✓	

Task 2 (10 marks)

This task is about understanding how to set up bookkeeping systems.

The business has the following assets and liabilities:

Assets and liabilities	£
Office furniture	6,250
Motor vehicles	24,000
Cash at bank	15,420
Receivables	9,530
Payables	4,350
Bank loan	10,800

(a) Show the accounting equation by inserting the appropriate figures. Do not use minus signs or brackets. **(3 marks)**

Assets £	Liabilities £	Capital £
		48,750

(b) Show the dual effect of each transaction by identifying the appropriate effect for each transaction in the table below. You can use each effect more than once. **(6 marks)**

Transaction	Dual effect
Sold goods for cash	3
Received cash from the owner of the business	4
Payment of goods purchased from a credit supplier using money in the bank account	2
Increase of a bank loan	1
Purchased goods on credit	5
Payment of an electricity invoice using money in the bank account	6

Description
Decrease in both an asset and a liability
Decrease in an asset and an increase in expenses
Increase in both an asset and income
Increase in both capital and an asset
Increase in a liability and expenses
Increase in both an asset and a liability

You have been asked to create a new general ledger account in your digital bookkeeping system for the following transaction.

BPP
LEARNING
MEDIA

(c) Identify the correct general ledger account for the following transaction.   (1 mark)

Rent incurred on the business premises.

	✓
Rent expense	✓
Trade payables	
Office furniture	
Sales	

Task 3 (10 marks)

This task is about processing customer transactions.

(a) Complete the following statement about prompt payment discounts by identifying ONE of the options below.   (1 mark)

A prompt payment discount is offered to customers _____

	✓
to encourage them to pay early.	✓
to encourage them to buy large quantities of goods.	

On 1 August Nixon Co had sent the following invoice to a credit customer:

INVOICE
Nixon Co
To: Grainger CateringCustomer ref GR87
Invoice number 8765
1 August 20XX
2,860 units............. Product H76
Price before discount: £2.00 per unit less 2% trade discount
£
Net amount after discount   5,605.60
VAT @ 20%   1,121.12
Total   6,726.72
Terms: Net monthly

A quarter of the goods arrived damaged. Grainger Catering returned these items to Nixon Co. Nixon agreed to give them a full refund for the damaged goods and issued a credit note on 16 August.

(b) Calculate the amounts to be included in the credit note.   (3 marks)

	£
Net amount after discount	
VAT @ 20%	
Total	

715

(c) Identify the daybook in which the credit note will be entered. (1 mark)

Daybook	✓
Sales daybook	
Sales returns daybook	
Purchases daybook	
Purchases returns daybook	
Discounts allowed daybook	
Discounts received daybook	

(d) Complete the entry in the daybook. (5 marks)

Date 20XX	Customer code	Customer	Credit note number	Total £	VAT £	Net £
		Grainger Catering	424			

Task 4 (10 marks)

This task is about processing customer transactions.

A receipt of £12,273 has been received from Falah Ltd. The following is an extract of the June sales listing for that customer from your digital bookkeeping system and the remittance advice.

June sales listing: Falah Ltd		
Date 20XX	Details	Amount £
5 June	Invoice: 3091	4,304
14 June	Credit note: 104	(914)
24 June	Invoice: 4001	5,110
25 June	Credit note: 109	(72)
30 June	Invoice: 4088	3,866

Remittance Advice: Falah Ltd To: Leon Services 30 June 20XX		
Date 20XX	Details	Amount £
6 June	Invoice: 3091	4,304
14 June	Credit note: 104	(914)
24 June	Credit note: 4001	5,110
25 June	Credit note: 109	(93)
30 June	Invoice: 4066	3,866

(a) Identify the discrepancies between the transactions recorded and the transactions on the remittance advice. (5 marks)

Invoice date	Details	£	Discrepancies
5 June	Invoice: 3091	4,304	
14 June	Credit note: 104	(914)	
24 June	Invoice: 4001	5,110	
25 June	Credit note: 109	(72)	
30 June	Invoice: 4088	3,866	

Options
Incorrect date
Incorrect invoice number
Incorrectly recorded
Incorrect amount
No discrepancies

(b) What will be the balance payable by Falah Ltd after their payment of £12,273 has been allocated to their account? (1 mark)

Balance on Falah Ltd's receivables account:

	✓
£21 underpaid	✓
£21 overpaid	

An invoice to supply goods for £6,620 plus VAT has been sent to GER Ltd offering a prompt payment discount of 4% for payment within 14 days.

(c) What will be the amount payable by GER Ltd if they pay within 14 days? (1 mark)

£ 7,626 24

Tariq Supplies

BACS Remittance Advice

To: Trentham Ltd

Date: 30 June

Amount: £10,402

Details:

- Part payment of the balance owed as at 1 June 20XX (£6,422)
- Part payment of invoice number 3093
- Full allocation of credit note 428

(d) Show the outstanding amount for each entry after the remittance has been allocated.
(3 marks)

Date	Detail	£	Outstanding amount £
1 June	Opening balance	7,450	
8 June	Invoice: 3093	6,782	
28 June	Credit note: 428	1,806	

Task 5 (10 marks)

This task is about processing supplier transactions.

The supplier invoice below has been checked, authorised and coded.

Tarant Training Co
Invoice no: 23103

To: Zeberdee Ltd   Date: 25 February 20XX

	£
Introduction to marketing – training course provided 17th and 18th February 20XX	2,583.90
VAT @ 20%	516.78
Total	3,100.68

Terms: Net monthly
Payment by BACS preferred

Checked by: MD	Authorised by: HK
General ledger code: 6590	Supplier code: TARA01

(a) Record the invoice in the bookkeeping system by:
- selecting the correct daybook
- making the necessary entries
- totalling the total, net and VAT columns   (7 marks)

Daybook	✓
Sales daybook	
Sales returns daybook	
Purchases daybook	
Purchases returns daybook	
Discounts allowed daybook	
Discounts received daybook	

Date 20XX	Supplier	Invoice number	Total £	VAT £	Net £
2 February	Johnson	8420	1,128.12	188.02	940.10
10 February	Fishpool & Sons	K/3455	4,213.08	702.18	3,510.90
12 February	Shapps Ltd	JH324	1,540.80	256.80	1,284.00
18 February	Abbas Co	GR3840	996.24	166.04	830.20
25 February	Tarant Training Co	23103			

The goods received note and credit note below relate to incorrect goods supplied to Aryi Ltd.

Aryi Ltd

Goods Received Note

1 September 20XX

The following goods have been received in our warehouse today from Papat Trading Ltd:

Product N3842, 200 items supplied 115 of these have been returned as they are not as ordered.

Net cost to us is £4.40 each.

Papat Trading Ltd

Credit Note: CN834

To: Aryi Ltd

Date: 4 September 20XX

	£
115 of Product N8342	506.00
VAT @ 20%	100.20
Total	605.00

(b)   **Identify THREE discrepancies in the credit note.**   (3 marks)

Discrepancy	✓
Quantity of items returned	
Product code	
Date of credit note	
Net amount	
VAT amount	
Total amount	

Task 6 (10 marks)

This task is about processing supplier transactions.

(a) **Identify which document would be used for each of the purposes below.**   (3 marks)

A document sent by the supplier to the customer when the customer returns goods in exchange for a refund.	Gap 1
A document sent by the supplier to accompany the goods despatched to the customer; states the product code, quantity supplied, together with the supplier/customer details.	Gap 2
A document created by a potential customer detailing their request for products to be supplied by another business; states the products and quantity required.	Gap 3

Gap 1 options	✓
Credit note	
Delivery note	
Purchase order	

Gap 2 options	✓
Credit note	
Delivery note	
Purchase order	

Gap 3 options	✓
Credit note	
Delivery note	
Purchase order	

It is the policy of Farringdon and Co to check statements of account when they are received, and only to include in the payment those transactions that are shown in the supplier's account in the payables ledger.

Below is the supplier account activity from the digital bookkeeping system.

Supplier activity report: Gem and Stones				
Date 20XX	Details	Debit £	Credit £	Balance £
1 May	Balance b/f		18,449	18,449
2 May	Credit note CN38	389		18,060
5 May	Bank payment	18,449		(389)
12 May	Invoice: 6931		890	501
21 May	Invoice: 6951		12,393	12,894
27 May	Invoice: 6982		3,392	16,286

(b) Identify the THREE items in the supplier's statement of account that should NOT be included in the payment because they are missing from the supplier activity report.
(3 marks)

Gem and Stones				
345 High Street, Tunbridge, TR3 93GF				
Date 20XX	Invoice/credit note number	Details	Amount £	✓
2 May	CN38	Good returned	389	
12 May	6931	Goods	890	
21 May	6951	Goods	12,393	
23 May	6977	Goods	5,380	
27 May	6982	Goods	3,392	
29 May	CN51	Good returned	634	
30 May	7002	Goods	1,352	

The two invoices below were received on 18 June from credit suppliers who offer a prompt payment discount.

Bainbridge Ltd
Invoice no: 3410
To: Phillip & Sons
Date: 16 June 20XX
£
34 × Product 921 @ £85 each   2,890.00
VAT @ 20%   578.00
Total   3,468.00
4% discount if payment received within 14 days of date of invoice

Noel plc
Invoice no: 4924
To: Phillip & Sons
Date: 17 June 20XX
£
420 × Product JH @ £5.30 each   2,226.00
VAT @ 20%   445.20
Total   2,671.20
5% discount if payment received within 10 days of date of invoice

(c) Calculate the amount to be paid to each supplier if the discount is take and identify the date (from the options below) by which the payment should be made. (4 marks)

Supplier	£	Date
Bainbridge Ltd		▼
Noel plc		▼

Date options
27 June 20XX
28 June 20XX
30 June 20XX
1 July 20XX

Task 7 (8 marks)

This task is about processing receipts and payments.

The amount shown below has been received from customers and the transaction is ready to be entered into the cash book module of your digital bookkeeping system.

Receipt 884
1 December 20XX
Cash sales for sales in the shop totalled £9,888 including VAT.

(a) Make the necessary entries in the cash book by:

- selecting the correct side of the cash book
- making the necessary entries. **(6 marks)**

Cash book	✓
Cash book – receipts	
Cash book – payments	

Date 20XX	Details	Total £	VAT £	Net £
	Option 1			

Option 1
Purchase tax
Credit sales
Cash sales
VAT

(b) Identify which document contains which piece of information. **(2 marks)**

Information	Document
Details of cheques received from credit customers	Gap 1
Details payments made directly from the business's bank account to a third party on a regular basis. The amount paid to each of the third parties varies in amount	Gap 2

Gap 1 options	✓
Direct debit schedule	
Cash receipt	
Paying in slip	
Cheque book stub	

Gap 2 options	✓
Direct debit schedule	
Cash receipt	
Paying in slip	
Cheque book stub	

Task 8 (6 marks)

This task is about processing receipts and payments.

An organisation keeps an analytical petty cash book.

On 30 December there was one final petty cash payment for the month to be recorded in the petty cash book. An amount of £100.80 including VAT had been made for catering expenses.

(a) **Identify the entry required in the petty cash book to record the closing balance on 31 December.** (2 marks)

VAT £	Net £

Before the petty cash payment in (a) was recorded, amounts totalling £305.88 had been entered into the food and drinks analysis column of the petty cash book.

(b) **Calculate the total of the food and drink expenses analysis column after the petty cash payment in (a) has been recorded.** (1 mark)

£	

After all the December petty cash payments had been made, an amount of £42.55 was left in the petty cash float. This agreed with the total of all payments now recorded in the petty cash book which was £186.56.

On 31 December the petty cash float was topped up to £300.

(c) **What will be the entry in the petty cash book to record this transaction?** (3 marks)

Details	Amount £	Debit ✓	Credit ✓
Gap 1			

Gap 1 options	✓
Cash receipts	
Credit sales	
Cash sales	
Cash from bank	

Task 9 (6 marks)

This task is about processing receipts and payments in a digital bookkeeping system.

Direct debit schedule

Detail:

Annually you are advised of the amount payable in respect of the building insurance on your business premises. The amount is payable monthly with the first of the new payments due on 20 March. On 1 March you received an email stating that the new monthly amount is £250.

VAT is not applicable.

Show the necessary entries in the cash book by
- selecting the correct side of the cash book
- making the necessary entries.

(6 marks)

Cash book	✓
Cash book – receipts	
Cash book – payments	

Date	Details	Total £	Frequency	Recurrences
	Option 1		Option 2	

Option 1 - Details
Cash receipts
Building insurance
Payments
Recurring payments

Option 2 - Frequency
Daily
Weekly
Monthly
Quarterly

Task 10 (10 marks)

This task is about transferring data from the books of prime entry.

These are the totals of the sales returns daybook at Marton Co.

Details	Total £	VAT £	Net £
Total	5,016	836	4,180

(a) Show the entries to be made in the general ledger accounts below. (9 marks)

Account name	Amount £	Debit ✓	Credit ✓
▼			
▼			
▼			

Account names options
Discounts allowed
Discounts received
Purchases
Purchase returns
Payables ledger control
Receivables ledger control
Sales
Sales returns
VAT

One of the entries in the discounts received daybook is a credit note received from Junipers Ltd for £70 plus VAT.

(b)   **Show the entry in the payables ledger.**

Account name	Amount £	Debit ✓	Credit ✓
▼			

Account names options
Discounts allowed
Discounts received
Junipers Ltd
Purchases
Purchase returns
Payables ledger control
Receivables ledger control
Sales
Sales returns
VAT

Task 11 (10 marks)

This task is about totalling and balancing ledger accounts.

The following account is in the general ledger at the close of day on 31 January.

Trade receivables

Date 20XX	Details	Amount £	Date 20XX	Details	Amount £
1 January	Balance b/f	12,760	15 January	Bank	10,540
20 January	Invoice	18,400			

(a)   **What will be the balance brought down on 31 January on the account?**   (2 marks)

Details	Amount £	Debit ✓	Credit ✓
Trade receivables			

The following account is in the electricity expense ledger at the close of day on 31 January.

(b)   **Complete the account below by:**

- **inserting the balance carried down together with date and details**
- **inserting the totals**
- **inserting the balance brought down together with date and details.**   (8 marks)

Electricity expense

Date 20XX	Details	Amount £	Date 20XX	Details	Amount £
1 January	Balance b/f	12,760	15 January	Bank	6,540
20 January	Invoice 2428	18,400	23 January	Credit note 153	453
	Total			Total	

Details options
Balance brought down
Balance carried down
Difference

Date options
1 January
1 February
31 January
28 February

BPP PRACTICE ASSESSMENT 2

INTRODUCTION TO BOOKKEEPING

ANSWERS

Introduction to Bookkeeping (ITBK)
BPP practice assessment 2

Task 1

(a)

Details the items requested by the customer; includes a product description, product code, quantity required and the agreed terms (price, discount if relevant).	Customer order
Detailing money paid in and paid out of the bank account for a given period, and stating the opening and closing balance at the start and end of the period.	Bank statement
Lists items sent to a business; includes customer and supplier details, date of despatch, the product code, the quantity, and the corresponding order number.	Delivery note
Details the items provided to credit customers; includes a description of the items supplied, product code, amount due including VAT/discounts where appropriate.	Invoice

(b)

Customer name	Customer account code
Hawkins Ltd	HAWKI01
Sanderstone & Co	SANDE02

(c)

	✓
Discount allowed daybook	✓
Discount received daybook	
Purchase daybook	
Sales daybook	

(d)

Statement	True ✓	False ✓
Some transactions can be entered in the general ledger as a single entry without giving rise to an error in the accounting records.		✓
In most digital accounting systems, transactions relating to receivables and payables are entered once in the sales daybook or purchases daybook. The relevant control account and ledger account are then automatically updated to reflect the postings.	✓	
In a manual accounting system, there is more scope for error as automatic entries and recurring entries are not possible.	✓	

All transactions must be entered in the general ledger using the double entry bookkeeping system. The dual effect is required to ensure entries are accurately and completely recorded.

Task 2

(a)

Assets £	Liabilities £	Capital £
55,200	15,150	40,050

Assets = £6,250 + £24,000 + £15,420 + £9,530 = £55,200

Liabilities = £4,350 + £10,800 = £15,150

Capital = assets − liabilities = £55,200 − £15,150 = £40,050

(b)

Transaction	Dual effect
Sold goods for cash	Increase in both an asset and income
Received cash from the owner of the business	Increase in both capital and an asset
Payment of goods purchased from a credit supplier using money in the bank account	Decrease in both an asset and a liability
Increase of a bank loan	Increase in both an asset and a liability
Purchased goods on credit	Increase in a liability and expenses
Payment of an electricity invoice using money in the bank account	Decrease in an asset and an increase in expenses

(c)

Transaction	✓
Rent expense	✓
Trade payables	
Office furniture	
Sales	

Task 3

(a)   A prompt payment discount is offered to customers

	✓
to encourage them to pay early.	✓
to encourage them to buy large quantities of goods.	

(b)

	£
Net amount after discount	1,401.40
VAT @ 20%	280.28
Total	1,681.68

(c)

Daybook	✓
Sales daybook	
Sales returns daybook	✓
Purchases daybook	
Purchases returns daybook	
Discounts allowed daybook	
Discounts received daybook	

(d)

Date 20XX	Customer code	Customer	Credit note number	Total £	VAT £	Net £
16 August	GR87	Grainger Catering	424	1,681.68	280.28	1,401.40

Task 4

(a)

Invoice date	Details	£	Discrepancies
5 June	Invoice: 3091	4,304	Incorrect date
14 June	Credit note: 104	(914)	No discrepancies
24 June	Invoice: 4001	5,110	Incorrectly recorded
25 June	Credit note: 109	(72)	Incorrect amount
30 June	Invoice: 4088	3,866	Incorrect invoice number

(b)

	✓
£21 underpaid	✓
£21 overpaid	

(c)

£	7,626.24

Working

Details	£
Net amount	6,620.00
VAT @ 20%	1,324.00
Total amount available	7,944.00
Less discount @ 4%	(317.76)
Amount payable	7,626.24

(d)

Date	Detail	£	Outstanding amount £
1 June	Opening balance	7,450	1,028
8 June	Invoice: 3093	6,782	996
28 June	Credit: 428	1,806	0

Workings

Details	£
Amount paid	10,402
Add credit note	1,806
Total amount available	12,208
Part payment of opening balance	(6,422)
Payment of invoice 3093 (balance)	5,786

Task 5

(a)

Daybook	✓
Sales daybook	
Sales returns daybook	
Purchases daybook	✓
Purchases returns daybook	
Discounts allowed daybook	
Discounts received daybook	

Date 20XX	Supplier	Invoice number	Total £	VAT £	Net £
2 February	Johnson	8420	1,128.12	188.02	940.10
10 February	Fishpool & Sons	K/3455	4,213.08	702.18	3,510.90
12 February	Shapps Ltd	JH324	1,540.80	256.80	1,284.00
18 February	Abbas Co	GR3840	996.24	166.04	830.20
25 February	Tarant Training Co	23103	3,100.68	516.78	2,583.90
			10,978.92	1,829.82	9,149.10

(b)

Discrepancy	✓
Quantity of items returned	
Product code	✓
Date of credit note	
Net amount	
VAT amount	✓
Total amount	✓

The goods received note shows the product code as N3842 whereas the credit note shows the product code as N8342.

The VAT should be calculated as £506.00 @ 20% = £101.20.

The total (gross) amount should be calculated as £506.00 plus £101.20 = £607.20.

It should also be noted that the cast of the invoice is incorrect (£506.00 plus £100.20 per the invoice = £606.20). However, the total per the invoice is incorrectly shown as £605.00.

Task 6

(a)

A document sent by the supplier to the customer when the customer returns goods in exchange for a refund.	Credit note
A document sent by the supplier to accompany the goods despatched to the customer; states the product code, quantity supplied, together with the supplier/customer details.	Delivery note
A document created by a potential customer detailing their request for products to be supplied by another business; states the products and quantity required.	Purchase order

(b)

Gem and Stones 345 High Street, Tunbridge, TR3 93GF				
Date 20XX	Invoice/credit note number	Details	Amount £	✓
2 May	CN38	Good returned	389	
12 May	6931	Goods	890	
21 May	6951	Goods	12,393	
23 May	6977	Goods	5,380	✓
27 May	6982	Goods	3,392	
29 May	CN51	Good returned	634	✓
30 May	7002	Goods	1,352	✓

(c)

Supplier	£	Date
Bainbridge Ltd	3,329.28	30 June 20XX
Noel plc	2,537.64	27 June 20XX

Workings:

Bainbridge Ltd:

£3,468.00 × 4% = £138.72

£3,468.00 − £138.72 = £3,329.28

Noel plc:

£2,671.20 × 5% = £133.56

£2,671.20 − £133.56 = £2,537.64

Task 7

(a)

Cash book	✓
Cash book – receipts	✓
Cash book – payments	

Date 20XX	Details	Total £	VAT £	Net £
1 December	Cash sales	9,888	1,648	8,240

(b)

Information	Document
Details of cheques received from credit customers	Paying in slip
Details payments made directly from the business's bank account to a third party on a regular basis. The amount paid to each of the third parties varies in amount	Direct debit schedule

Task 8

(a)

VAT £	Net £
16.80	84.00

(b)

£	389.88

Working:

£305.88 + £84.00 = £389.88

Note that the expense is recorded at the net amount.

(c)

Details	Amount £	Debit ✓	Credit ✓
Cash from bank	257.45	✓	

Working:

£300.00 – £42.55 = £257.45

Task 9

Cash book	✓
Cash book – receipts	
Cash book – payments	✓

Date	Details	Total £	Frequency	Recurrences
20 March	Business insurance	250	Monthly	12

Task 10

(a)

Account name	Amount £	Debit ✓	Credit ✓
Sales returns	4,180	✓	
VAT	836	✓	
Receivables ledger control	5,016		✓

(b)

Account name	Amount £	Debit ✓	Credit ✓
Junipers Ltd	84	✓	

Task 11

(a)

Details	Amount £	Debit ✓	Credit ✓
Trade receivables	20,620	✓	

(b) **Electricity expense**

Date 20XX	Details	Amount £	Date 20XX	Details	Amount £
1 January	Balance b/f	12,760	15 January	Bank	6,540
20 January	Invoice 2428	18,400	23 January	Credit note 153	453
			31 January	Balance c/d	24,167
	Total	31,160		Total	31,160
1 February	Balance b/d	24,167			

BPP PRACTICE ASSESSMENT 3

INTRODUCTION TO BOOKKEEPING

Time allowed: 1.5 hours

Introduction to Bookkeeping (ITBK)
BPP practice assessment 3

Introduction

The tasks in this assessment are set in different business situations where the following apply:

- Businesses use a variety of bookkeeping systems.
- Double entry takes place in the general ledger.
- The VAT rate is 20%.

Task 1 (10 marks)

This task is about manual and digital bookkeeping systems.

(a) **Identify which document or report would be used for each of the purposes below.**

(4 marks)

To summarise assets and liabilities and report the business's financial position at the end of the accounting period.	Gap 1
To identify whether or not there is an imbalance in debit and credit entries in the nominal ledger.	Gap 2
To summarise income and expenses for a period.	Gap 3
To identify which credit suppliers are due for payment.	Gap 4

Gap 1 options	✓
Statement of financial position	✓
Statement of profit or loss	
Trade payables listing	
Trial balance	

Gap 2 options	✓
Statement of financial position	
Statement of profit or loss	
Trade payables listing	
Trial balance	✓

Gap 3 options	✓
Statement of financial position	
Statement of profit or loss	✓
Trade payables listing	
Trial balance	

Gap 4 options	✓
Statement of financial position	
Statement of profit or loss	
Trade payables listing	✓
Trial balance	

A new business has allocated a customer account code to each customer in the receivables ledger, as shown below. The code is made up of the first four letters of the customer's name, followed by the number of the ledger page allocated to each customer in that alphabetical group.

Customer name	Customer account code
Aspen Ltd	ASPE01
Attwood Ltd	ATTW02
Dunston Designs	DUNS01
Genie Products	GENI01
Latham Ltd	LATH01
Pemberton Ltd	PEMB01
Penn Ltd	PENN02

The two new customer accounts shown below have been added to the receivables ledger and need to be allocated a customer account code.

(b) **Insert the relevant account codes for each customer.** (2 marks)

General plc   Account code: GENE02

Multipack Ltd   Account code: MULT01

(c) **Identify the book of prime entry being described in the statement below.** (1 mark)

A daybook detailing goods the business has returned to its credit suppliers.

	✓
Discount allowed daybook	
Discount received daybook	
Purchase returns daybook	
Sales returns daybook	✓

(d) **Identify whether the following statements regarding bookkeeping systems are true or false.** (3 marks)

Statement	True ✓	False ✓
A digital accounting system can be used to generate financial documents such as sales invoices and credit notes.	✓	
In both a digital accounting system and a manual accounting system the bookkeeper has to manually total the ledger accounts.		✓
CSV files enable information to be imported into a digital accounting system.	✓	

Task 2 (10 marks)

This task is about principles of double-entry bookkeeping.

The following accounts are in the bookkeeping system.

(a)   **Identify the classification of each account.**   **(4 marks)**

Bank overdraft	Gap 1
Contributions made by the owners of the business	Gap 2
Bank interest earned by the business	Gap 3
Payroll liability: HMRC	Gap 4

Gap 1 options	✓
Capital	
Liability	✓
Income	
Expense	

Gap 2 options	✓
Capital	✓
Liability	
Income	✗
Expense	

Gap 3 options	✓
Capital	
Liability	
Income	✓
Expense	

Gap 4 options	✓
Capital	
Liability	✗
Income	
Expense	✓

The liabilities accounts total £210,042 and the capital account shows a balance of £394,425.

(b)   **Calculate the amount of assets in the business. Do NOT use a minus sign or brackets.**
                                                                           (1 mark)

£	

The transactions below have been entered into the bookkeeping system.

(c)   **Identify the dual effect of each transaction by dragging the appropriate description into the table below. You should ignore VAT in this task.**   **(5 marks)**

Transaction	Dual effect
Received money from a credit customer which increased the bank balance	(2)
Received a discount from a credit supplier in part settlement of a liability	(5)
Sold goods for cash	(4)
Owner contributed capital to the business in the form of cash which reduced a bank overdraft	(3)
Paid credit suppliers from a positive bank balance	(1)

Description
Decrease in both assets and liabilities
Increase in income and decrease in liabilities
Increase in capital and decrease in liabilities
Both increase and decrease in assets
Increase in income and increase in assets

Task 3 (10 marks)

This task is about processing customer invoices or credit notes and entering in daybooks.

Monty Ltd had sent TBD Ltd the following sales invoice:

Monty Ltd	
To: TBD Ltd 2 November 20XX Invoice no: 3521	
	£
70 units Product G350	175.00
VAT @ 20%	35.00
Total	210.00
Terms: Net monthly; 4% prompt payment discount for payment within 10 days	

On 6 November TBD Ltd paid the invoice taking advantage of the prompt payment discount offered.

(a) **Calculated the amounts to be included in the credit note in respect of the prompt payment discount.** (3 marks)

	£
Net amount	7
VAT @ 20%	1·4
Total	8·

(b) **Identify the daybook in which the credit note will be entered.** (1 mark)

Daybook	✓
Sales daybook	
Sales returns daybook	
Purchases daybook	
Purchases returns daybook	
Discounts allowed daybook	✓
Discounts received daybook	

(c)   Complete the entry for the credit note in the daybook.   (4 marks)

Date 20XX	Customer code	Customer	Credit note number	Total £	VAT £	Net £	G352 £	G350 £	G351 £
7 Nov	TB01	TBD Ltd	CR84						

(d)   Identify the type of discount being described by the statements below.   (2 marks)

Description	
Offered to encourage customers to enter into the transaction.	Gap 1
Offered to encourage customers to settle the amount due early.	Gap 2

Gap 1 options	✓
Bulk discount	
Prompt payment discount	—
Trade discount	

Gap 2 options	✓
Bulk discount	
Prompt payment discount	╷
Trade discount	

Task 4 (10 marks)

This task is about processing receipts from customers.

Bevan Ltd has received a cheque for £1,561.80 from Ellis Ltd in full settlement of the two invoices and credit note below.

Bevan Ltd	
To: Ellis Ltd	
6 January 20XX	
Invoice No: 8499	
	£
205 units Product MH4	881.50
VAT @ 20%	176.30
Total	1,057.80
Terms: Net monthly	

Bevan Ltd	
To: Ellis Ltd	
10 January 20XX	
Invoice No: 8500	
	£
120 units Product GL2	420.00
VAT @ 20%	84.00
Total	504.00
Terms: Net monthly	

Bevan Ltd	
To: Ellis Ltd	
15 January 20XX	
Credit note No: 92	
	£
36 units Product MH4	154.80
VAT @ 20%	30.96
Total	185.76
Terms: Net monthly	

(a) Complete the following statement about the accuracy of the amount received by selecting the appropriate option in each gap below. **(2 marks)**

Ellis Ltd has.......	
so	

Gap 1 options	✓
underpaid the amount owing	
overpaid the amount owing	
paid the correct amount	

Gap 2 options	✓
a request for a further payment should be made.	
there is no balance outstanding.	
a refund should be offered.	

Mendoza plc has offered a customer a 3% discount for payment of all the outstanding invoices detailed below, by the end of the month.

(b) Calculate the amount that should be paid by the end of the month to settle:

- each invoice
- the total of all the invoices. **(4 marks)**

Outstanding invoices	Total £	VAT £	Net £	Amount to be paid by the end of the month
4752	2,478.00	413.00	2,065.00	
4758	1,194.00	199.00	995.00	
4766	804.00	134.00	670.00	

Seema Ltd has received a cheque for £3,786.82 and the remittance advice below from a customer. The customer's terms of payment are net monthly.

Remittance advice	
Invoice	£
5034	536.21
5042	892.36
5050	1,592.43
5059	765.82
Total	3,786.82

Company policy is to allocate any underpayment as a part payment and to query any overpayment.

(c) Allocate the amount received in the customer report below, by selecting the appropriate action to take for each transaction. **(4 marks)**

Transaction type	Details	Amount £	Action
Balance b/f		1,420.00	Gap 1
Invoice 5050	Delivery note 3009	1,689.43	Gap 2
Invoice 5059	Delivery note 3015	850.75	Gap 3
Credit note 209	Re overcharge in invoice 5050	97.00	Gap 4

Gap 1 options	✓
Allocate full amount	
Allocate part payment	
Query overpayment	

Gap 2 options	✓
Allocate full amount	
Allocate part payment	
Query overpayment	

Gap 3 options	✓
Allocate full amount	
Allocate part payment	
Query overpayment	

Gap 4 options	✓
Allocate full amount	
Allocate part payment	
Query overpayment	

Task 5 (10 marks)

This task is about processing supplier transactions.

Shown below is a statement of account received from a credit supplier, and the supplier's account as shown in the payables ledger of Trappic Ltd.

> Lemonfresh Ltd
> 90 West Street
> Arbuckle
> AR4 8AM

To: Trappic Ltd
8 Highview Road
Arbuckle
AR7 4LX

STATEMENT OF ACCOUNT

Date 20XX	Invoice Number	Details	Invoice amount £	Cheque amount £	Balance £
1 June	1267	Goods	180		180
3 June	1387	Goods	230		410
7 June	1422	Goods	290		700
10 June	1498	Goods	800		1,500
16 June		Cheque		510	990

Lemonfresh Ltd

Date 20XX	Details	Amount £	Date 20XX	Details	Amount £
16 June	Bank	510	1 June	Invoice 1267	180
16 June	Credit note 535	10	3 June	Invoice 1387	230
			7 June	Invoice 1422	290

(a)   Which item is missing from the statement of account from Lemonfresh Ltd?   (2 marks)

Option	✓
Cheque for £510	
Credit note 535	
Invoice 1267	
Invoice 1387	
Invoice 1422	
Invoice 1498	

(b)   Which item is missing from the supplier's account in Trappic Ltd's payables ledger?
(2 marks)

Option	✓
Cheque for £510	
Credit note 535	
Invoice 1267	
Invoice 1387	
Invoice 1422	
Invoice 1498	

(c)   Assuming any differences between the statement of account from Lemonfresh Ltd and the supplier's account in Trappic Ltd's payables ledger are simply due to omission errors, what is the amount owing to Lemonfresh Ltd?   (2 marks)

£ [   ]

Trappic Ltd prepares a remittance advice note in respect of Lemonfresh Ltd.

(d)   Which of the following statements is true?   (1 mark)

	✓
The remittance advice note will be sent to the customer to advise them of the amount being paid.	
The remittance advice note will be sent to the supplier's bank to advise them of the amount being paid.	
The remittance advice note will be sent to the supplier to advise them of the amount being paid.	
The remittance advice note will be sent to the accounts department at Lemonfresh Ltd to request that a cheque is raised.	

An invoice dated 18 June 20XX has been received from Lemonfresh Ltd for £760.00 plus VAT. A prompt payment discount of 5% is offered for payment within 10 days.

(e) Complete the table below:
- Enter the name of the supplier
- Calculate the amount to be paid to Lemonfresh Ltd if the discount is taken and
- Show the date by which Lemonfresh Ltd should receive the payment.   (3 marks)

Supplier	Amount £	Date by which payment should be received by supplier
Gap 1		Gap 2

Gap 1 options	✓
Trappic Ltd	
Lemonfresh Ltd	

Gap 2 options	✓
18 June 20XX	
27 June 20XX	
28 June 20XX	
29 June 20XX	

Task 6 (10 marks)

This task is about processing supplier transactions.

The invoice and purchase order below relate to goods received from XYZ Ltd.

Invoice

```
              XYZ Ltd
VAT Registration number 963 5353 01

           Invoice No. 8753
To: B Smith              19 May 20XX
                                  £
50 units, product code 5357 @
    £5 each                  250.00
Trade discount @10%           25.00
Total                        225.00

  Terms: 3% discount for payment within
                10 days
```

Purchase order

```
              B Smith
            Order PO432

To: XYZ Ltd              13 May 20XX

Please supply:

100 units, product code 5357 @ £5 each less
10% trade discount

As agreed, terms of payment are 3% discount
      for payment within 10 days.
```

(a) Identify any discrepancies on the invoice by drawing a line from each left hand box to the appropriate right hand box. **(4 marks)**

Terms of payment	Not shown on invoice
VAT rate	Incorrectly shown on invoice
Trade discount	Correctly shown on invoice
Quantity	

The invoice below has been received from Clinton plc.

Invoice

Clinton plc
VAT Registration number 896 5421 01

Invoice No. 6532

To: B Smith   19 May 20XX

	£
5 units, product code 952 @ £15.35 each	76.75
VAT @ 20%	15.35
Total	92.10

Terms: 4% discount for payment in
10 days

(b) Record the invoice in the appropriate daybook by:

- Selecting the correct daybook title; and
- Making the necessary entries. **(5 marks)**

Daybook	✓
Sales daybook	
Sales returns daybook	
Purchases daybook	
Purchases returns daybook	
Discounts allowed daybook	
Discounts received daybook	

Date 20XX	Details	Invoice number	Total £	VAT £	Net £
19 May	Option 1	6532			

Details
B Smith
Clinton plc

The invoice below has been received from Keys Ltd.

Invoice

Keys Ltd
VAT Registration number 324 5361 04

Invoice No. 8592

To: B Smith   22 June 20XX
                                                                          £

5 units, product code B84 @ £16.94 each   84.70

VAT @ 20%   16.94

Total   101.64

Terms: 5% discount for payment in
14 days

B Smith does not take advantage of the prompt payment discount offered.

(c)   **What is the total amount to be recorded in the purchases daybook in respect of this invoice?**   (1 mark)

£	

Task 7 (8 marks)

This task is about processing transactions in the cash book.

The cash book should be treated as part of the double entry booking system.

These are totals of the cash book at the end of the month.

Cash book

Debit side					Credit side				
Cash £	Bank £	VAT £	Trade receivables £	Cash sales £	Cash £	Bank £	VAT £	Trade payables £	Cash purchases £
680	8,255	–	6,190	–	680	8,255	59	5,450	295

What will be the entries in the general ledger? (8 marks)

Account name	Amount £	Debit ✓	Credit ✓
VAT	59		✓
Payables ledger control	5,450		✓
Cash purchases	295		✓
Receivables ledger control	6,190	✓	

Task 8 (6 marks)

This task is about processing transactions in the petty cash book.

Complete the petty cash book by totalling the petty cash book and inserting the balance carried down at 31 October. (6 marks)

Petty cash book

Date 20XX	Details	Amount £	Date 20XX	Details	Amount £	VAT £	Motor expenses £	Office expenses £
24 Oct	Balance b/f	37.60	27 Oct	Postage stamps	5.45			5.45
24 Oct	Cash from bank	72.40	31 Oct	Motor repairs	42.50		42.50	
			31 Oct	Stationery	18.60	3.10		15.50
			31 Oct	Balance c/d				
	Total			Total				

Task 9 (6 marks)

This task is about processing recurring entries.

A new bank payment has been authorised as shown in the note below.

> I have today authorised a quarterly standing order relating to water rates paid to GB Council.
>
> Please set up a recurring entry to pay the total amount of £3,400 in equal instalments of £850, starting on 28 February.
>
> The transaction is exempt from VAT.
>
> John Hughes
>
> 15 February 20XX

(a) **Set up the recurring entry.** (5 marks)

Transaction type	Details	Start date 20XX	Frequency	Recurrences	Amount £	VAT code
Bank payment	Option 1	28 February	Option 2	4	850	Option 3

Option 1
220 – Bank
240 – Cash
960 – Water rates
980 – Rent

Option 2
Weekly
Bi-weekly
Monthly
Quarterly ✓

Option 3
VAT1 – Exempt
VAT2 – 0%
VAT3 – 5%
VAT 4 – 20%

(b)   Indicate whether the payment made in respect of water rates is a debit or credit entry in the cash book.   (1 mark)

Debit	Credit
✓	✓
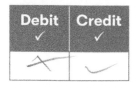

Task 10 (10 marks)

This task is about transferring data from the books of prime entry.

These are the totals of the discounts allowed daybook at the end of the month.

Discounts allowed daybook

Details	Total £	VAT £	Net £
Totals	378	63	315

(a)   **What will be the entries in the general ledger?**   (9 marks)

Account name	Amount £	Debit ✓	Credit ✓
Option 1	378		✓
Option 2	63	✓	
Option 3	315	✓	

Option 1
Discounts allowed ✓
Discounts received
Payables ledger control
Purchases
Purchases returns
Receivables ledger control
Sales
Sales returns
VAT

Option 2
Discounts allowed
Discounts received
Payables ledger control
Purchases
Purchases returns
Receivables ledger control ✓
Sales
Sales returns
VAT ✓

Option 3
Discounts allowed
Discounts received
Payables ledger control
Purchases
Purchases returns
Receivables ledger control
Sales
Sales returns
VAT

One of the entries in the discounts allowed daybook is for a credit note sent to Samuel Smith for £112 plus VAT.

(b) **What will be the amount entered in the receivables ledger in respect of this transaction?** (1 mark)

Account name	Amount £	Debit ✓	Credit ✓
Samuel Smith	134.4		✓

Task 11 (10 marks)

This task is about totalling and balancing ledger accounts.

The following two accounts are in the general ledger at close of day on 31 January.

Loan from bank

Date 20XX	Details	Amount £	Date 20XX	Details	Amount £
15 Jan	Bank	3,050	1 Jan	Balance b/f	36,525
31 Jan	Bal c/d	53,475	31 Jan	Bank	20,000

Motor Vehicles

Date 20XX	Details	Amount £	Date 20XX	Details	Amount £
1 Jan	Balance b/f	32,900	30 Jan	Journal	500
8 Jan	Bank	2,500			

(a) What will be the balance brought down at 1 February on each account? (2 marks)

Account	Balance b/d at 1 February
Loan from bank	53,475
Motor Vehicles	34,900

The following account is in the receivables ledger at the close of day on 31 January.

(b) Complete the account below by: (8 marks)

- Inserting the balance carried down together with date and details.
- Inserting the totals.
- Inserting the balance brought down together with date and details.

Trevor Tate

Date 20XX	Details	Amount £	Date 20XX	Details	Amount £
1 Jan	Balance b/f	9,899	22 Jan	Bank	5,780
11 Jan	Invoice 155	1,001	29 Jan	Credit Note C15	714
			Option 1 31 Jan	Option 2 Bal c/d	5,834
	Total	10,900		Total	10,900
Option 1	Option 2				

Option 1
1 Feb
31 Jan

Option 2
Balance b/d
Balance c/d
Trevor Tate

BPP PRACTICE ASSESSMENT 3

INTRODUCTION TO BOOKKEEPING

ANSWERS

Introduction to Bookkeeping (ITBK)
BPP practice assessment 3

Task 1

(a)

To summarise assets and liabilities and report the business's financial position at the end of the accounting period.	Statement of financial position
To identify whether or not there is an imbalance in debit and credit entries in the nominal ledger.	Trial balance
To summarise income and expenses for a period.	Statement of profit or loss
To identify which credit suppliers are due for payment.	Trade payables listing

(b)

General plc Account code: GENE02

Multipack Ltd Account code: MULT01

(c)

	✓
Discount allowed daybook	
Discount received daybook	
Purchase returns daybook	✓
Sales returns daybook	

(d)

Statement	True ✓	False ✓
A digital accounting system can be used to generate financial documents such as sales invoices and credit notes.	✓	
In both a digital accounting system and a manual accounting system the bookkeeper has to manually total the ledger accounts.		✓
CSV files enable information to be imported into a digital accounting system.	✓	

Task 2

(a)

Bank overdraft	Liability
Contributions made by the owners of the business	Capital
Bank interest earned by the business	Income
Payroll liability: HMRC	Liability

(b)

£	604,467

Working: £210,042 plus £394,425 = £604,467.

(c)

Transaction	Dual effect
Received money from a credit customer which increased the bank balance	Both increase and decrease in assets
Received a discount from a credit supplier in part settlement of a liability	Increase in income and decrease in liabilities
Sold goods for cash	Increase in income and increase in assets
Owner contributed capital to the business in the form of cash which reduced a bank overdraft	Increase in capital and decrease in liabilities
Paid credit suppliers from a positive bank balance	Decrease in both assets and liabilities

Task 3

(a)

	£
Net amount	7.00
VAT @ 20%	1.40
Total	8.40

Working:

£175.00 × 4% = £7.00

£35.00 × 4% = £1.40

£210.00 × 4% = £8.40.

(b)

Daybook	✓
Sales daybook	
Sales returns daybook	
Purchases daybook	
Purchases returns daybook	
Discounts allowed daybook	✓
Discounts received daybook	

(c)

Date 20XX	Customer code	Customer	Credit note number	Total £	VAT £	Net £	G352 £	G350 £	G351 £
7 Nov	TB01	TBD Ltd	CR84	8.40	1.40	7.00		7.00	

(d)

Description	
Offered to encourage customers to enter into the transaction.	Trade discount
Offered to encourage customers to settle the amount due early.	Prompt payment discount

Task 4

(a)

Ellis Ltd has.......	overpaid the amount owing
so	a refund should be offered.

(b)

Outstanding invoices	Total £	VAT £	Net £	Amount to be paid by the end of the month
4752	2,478.00	413.00	2,065.00	2,403.66
4758	1,194.00	199.00	995.00	1,158.18
4766	804.00	134.00	670.00	779.88
				4,341.72

Workings

£2,478.00 × 97% = £2,403.66

£1,194.00 × 97% = £1,158.18

£804.00 × 97% = £779.88

(c)

Transaction type	Details	Amount £	Action
Balance b/f		1,420.00	Query over payment
Invoice 5050	Delivery note 3009	1,689.43	Allocate full amount
Invoice 5059	Delivery note 3015	850.75	Allocate part payment
Credit note 209	Re overcharge in invoice 5050	97.00	Allocate full amount

Workings:

Balance b/d = £536.21 + £892.36 = £1,428.57, therefore overpaid by £8.57

Invoice 5050 £1,689.43 less credit note 209 for £97.00 is £1,592.43 therefore, allocate full amount

Invoice 5059 only £765.82 was paid instead of £850.75, therefore allocate part payment

---

Task 5

(a)

Credit note 535

(b)

Invoice 1498

(c)

£	980

Workings

£990 − £10 = £980

(d)

	✓
The remittance advice note will be sent to the customer to advise them of the amount being paid	
The remittance advice note will be sent to the supplier's bank to advise them of the amount being paid	
The remittance advice note will be sent to the supplier to advise them of the amount being paid	✓
The remittance advice note will be sent to the accounts department at Lemonfresh Ltd to request that a cheque is raised	

(e)

Supplier	Amount £	Date by which payment should be received by supplier
Lemonfresh Ltd	866.40	28 June 20XX

Working

VAT = £760 × 20% = £152, Gross amount = £760 + £152 = £912,

Gross less discount = £912 × 95% = £866.40

Task 6

(a)

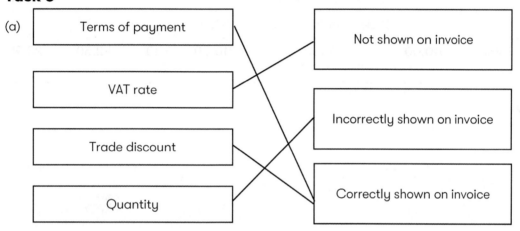

(b)

Purchases daybook

Date 20XX	Details	Invoice number	Total £	VAT £	Net £
19 May	Clinton plc	6532	92.10	15.35	76.75

(c)

£	101.64

Task 7

Account name	Amount £	Debit ✓	Credit ✓
VAT	59	✓	
Payables ledger control	5,450	✓	
Cash purchases	295	✓	
Receivables ledger control	6,190		✓

ANSWERS

Task 8

Petty cash book

Date 20XX	Details	Amount £	Date 20XX	Details	Amount £	VAT £	Motor expenses £	Office expenses £
24 Oct	Balance b/f	37.60	27 Oct	Postage stamps	5.45			5.45
24 Oct	Cash from bank	72.40	31 Oct	Motor repairs	42.50		42.50	
			31 Oct	Stationery	18.60	3.10		15.50
			31 Oct	Balance c/d	43.45			
	Total	110.00		Total	110.00	3.10	42.50	20.95

Task 9

(a)

Transaction type	Details	Start date 20XX	Frequency	Recurrences	Amount £	VAT code
Bank payment	960 – Water rates	28 February	Quarterly	4	850	VAT1 – Exempt

(b)

Debit ✓	Credit ✓
	✓

Task 10

(a)

Account name	Amount £	Debit ✓	Credit ✓
Discounts allowed	315	✓	
VAT	63	✓	
Receivables ledger control	378		✓

(b)

Account name	Amount £	Debit ✓	Credit ✓
Samuel Smith	134.40		✓

Working

£112 + (£112 × 20%) = £134.40

Task 11

(a)

Account	Balance b/d at 1 February
Loan from bank	53,475
Motor Vehicles	34,900

Workings

Loan from bank

Date 20XX	Details	Amount £	Date 20XX	Details	Amount £
15 Jan	Bank	3,050	1 Jan	Balance b/f	36,525
31 Jan	Balance c/d	53,475	31 Jan	Bank	20,000
	Total	56,525		Total	56,525

Motor vehicles

Date 20XX	Details	Amount £	Date 20XX	Details	Amount £
1 Jan	Balance b/f	32,900	30 Jan	Journal	500
8 Jan	Bank	2,500	31 Jan	Balance c/d	34,900
	Total	35,400		Total	35,400

(b) **Trevor Tate**

Date 20XX	Details	Amount £	Date 20XX	Details	Amount £
1 Jan	Balance b/f	9,899	22 Jan	Bank	5,780
11 Jan	Invoice 155	1,001	29 Jan	Credit Note C15	714
			31 Jan	Balance c/d	4,406
	Total	10,900		Total	10,900
1 Feb	Balance b/d	4,406			